deep as the sea

Letters to Survivors of Trauma

Timothy C. Bourman

D0584505

NORTHWESTERN PUBLISHING HOUSE
Milwaukee, Wisconsin

Second edition, 2024

Design and layout: Lynda Williams
Image: iStock

Northwestern Publishing House
N16W23379 Stone Ridge Dr., Waukesha, WI 53188
www.nph.net
© 2021 Northwestern Publishing House
Published 2022
Printed in the United States of America
ISBN 978-0-8100-3152-4
ISBN 978-0-8100-3153-1 (e-book)

24 25 26 27 28 29 30 31 32 33   10 9 8 7 6 5 4 3 2 1

Dedication

To my Father in heaven who loved me with his only Son. To the only love of my life, Amanda Lynn, who held my hand and prayed with me. To my three daughters—Tayley, Brooke, and Felicity— who are God's precious gifts to me. To James and Hope, my parents, who turned their lives upside down just to remain with me. To my church, Sure Foundation, that shows me every day what grace really is by continuing to want me to be their pastor.

contents

prologue

Dear Survivor,

I remember waking up in bed wishing that such a thing as a pensieve[1] really did exist. That is the only way I can describe the moment. I wanted to take a wand just like Harry Potter did and simply remove the traumatic memories swirling around in my head. In fact, with all my heart I wanted to draw the memory right out and put it into that magic, fantastical pensieve so I could review it at my leisure or, even better, never examine the memory again. Just days earlier, I had literally stared at my own death and survived. As I woke up, I was overwhelmed by the memories, and there was no pensieve. I squeezed my eyes shut and held my wife, wishing for a brief moment that I did not exist. I was so startled and overwhelmed by the moment that I immediately began a desperate search to find a trusted resource that would explain the betrayal of my mind and how God intended to heal it.

I started looking for Christian resources that spoke of post-traumatic stress disorder (PTSD) and trauma. I wondered if there might be a devotional, blog, or podcast that was able to speak to my pain. I could not find blogs specifically written for the survivor of trauma, but I did find various articles written by Christians on the topic. I eagerly devoured them, wanting more. I scoured the internet looking for resources. I found tremendous devotionals and books for people grieving a death. However, the same was not true for those who had faced death and gone on living. I found a few pamphlets for the divorced, a handful for childhood sexual abuse, and one or two about domestic abuse. I finally gave up. In my journey to find spiritual resources for trauma, I had come up nearly empty at a time when I yearned for a word from God.

Even as I squeezed my eyes shut, God was already purposing good to come out of what I had suffered. This experience eventually moved me to fill the void I had encountered with this anthology of letters. I wanted to provide the resource I had felt was missing for survivors when I needed it most.

As I wrote these letters, I kept asking, "What would I share with myself, the me who squeezed his eyes shut, the me who was overwhelmed by the memories?" But I knew that my experience was as one of a kind as everyone else's. I wanted others to ask the same questions I was asking. I asked other survivors to respond to my letters, to tweak them, deepen them, and help me write with even more power. I sat with them and listened to their stories, their tears, and the hope they had in God. Some of them had suffered sexual trauma like rape or sexual abuse as a child. Some had been to war or suffered horrible accidents that left them not only physically but also spiritually and emotionally wounded. I spoke with survivors about the trauma of taking the life of another or identifying the dead body of their own child. I asked them to share their hardwon wisdom to shape and form my collection of letters. As a team brought together by the Spirit himself, we have knit together this collection of letters. While the survivors who helped with this book will remain nameless, their stories and their impact are on every page and between each line of this book.

This is not a devotional. I am not going to offer little one-page reads or short reflections. The letters go deeper than that. The intended audience and the subject matter call for something more than surface-level treatment. These letters are not for those who are bored with life or are just looking for a short encouragement from God's Word. You can go to a multitude of other places if you are looking for something like that. Instead, this book is specifically written for you, the survivor of trauma. This book is for the veteran with PTSD but also for survivors of a mass shooting, sexual assault, horrific accident, childhood abuse, natural disaster, 9/11, and so many other kinds of trauma. If your heart and soul have been broken by the world, I have written these letters to you. These are survivor letters.

I wish I would have had these letters that day when I squeezed my eyes shut. Today, if I had a choice to give myself Harry Potter's pensieve or *Deep as the Sea,* the choice would be easy. I would hand myself *Deep as the Sea* and say, "You are not alone. There are others. Your God hides himself in Jesus who died for you. The Father will send his Spirit, the Comforter, to help and to heal. He is faithful."

Trauma Defined

You have suffered a grievous wound. In fact, your wound may be as deep as the sea. I say that not so you become hopeless. God's love for us in Christ is even deeper than the sea. I tell you this so that you are patient with God's healing. *Trauma* is a word that comes from the Greek language. It simply means "wound."

The American Psychological Association (APA) has further narrowed the meaning of trauma. Iterations of the *Diagnostic and Statistical Manual of Mental Disorders* (DSM) have proved invaluable in developing diagnostic criteria for trauma. However, it was the Substance Abuse and Mental Health Services Administration (SAMHSA) that gathered a panel of experts on trauma. Their working definition of trauma has become pervasive in medical literature. According to this panel:

> Individual trauma results from an event, series of events, or set of circumstances that is experienced by an individual as physically or emotionally harmful or life-threatening and that has lasting adverse effects on the individual's functioning and mental, physical, social, emotional, or spiritual well-being.[2]

Key to this working definition are its three components. First comes an *event*. Typically, this event will cause the individual to think that his or her life is ending. However, this definition does not exclude other circumstances.[3] Second, trauma depends on the person's *experience*. People experience events in different ways. For example, a hurricane in Haiti may have proved traumatic to one person, but to another person the hurricane just "blew past" with much less emotional impact. Finally, according to this definition, trauma always comes with adverse *effects*.[4]

The effects of trauma take many forms. In her book *Trauma and Recovery*, Judith Herman groups those effects into three categories: intrusion, constriction, and hyperarousal. I will supplement her list with a fourth: spiritual loss. You may experience some of these effects or all of them.

Intrusion

The first effect of trauma listed by Herman is intrusion. Trauma often causes intrusion because of the special nature of traumatic memories. Traumatic memories have the extraordinary power of being ever-present. When you're awake, traumatic memories may break into the present in the form of flashbacks. Everyday events in your life may trigger these flashbacks. When asleep, traumatic memories may intrude in the form of nightmares. It may seem that you are constantly reliving the nightmare of your trauma.

Traumatic memories have this ever-present power because of their unique qualities. Psychologists have discovered that traumatic memories are not encoded like everyday memories. They are not woven into the fabric of our personal stories. Instead, they are "frozen and wordless."[5] Traumatic memories are filled with smells and images and intense feelings, but they have no narrative quality. They do not speak; they only haunt.

Your traumatic memories might be so intrusive and intense that you may experience rage and terror at levels the people around you cannot understand. You may begin to avoid people, places, and anything else that might trigger memories of the trauma.[6]

Constriction

Constriction basically means falling into a state of despair. This marks the difference between a bad memory and a traumatic memory. Constriction has to do with the loss of personal agency: your ability to exert yourself in the world. For some, 9/11 is not a traumatic memory because they retained their personal agency. They were able to run away from the scene and save themselves.[7] Trauma for most people, however, almost always includes the complete loss of personal agency. The survivor is unable to fight or run. This is the purest kind of victim. In the words of a rape survivor, "I could not scream. I could not move. I was paralyzed . . . like a rag doll."[8] During the trauma, since the survivor cannot run or fight, the body constricts in order to save energy for the final struggle to survive.

Constriction may cause a kind of learned helplessness or hopelessness in your heart. You may feel like giving up on your future life or find it completely meaningless.

Hyperarousal

The third effect of trauma is hyperarousal. Hyperarousal is the "cardinal symptom" of PTSD.[9] After a traumatic event, your psychology and physiology may conspire to make your post-traumatic life almost unbearable. The smallest sounds may be interpreted by your brain as threatening. You may feel jumpy and experience increased heart rate, elevated blood pressure, and the release of stress hormones. Everything may seem to be a danger. You may have trouble relaxing and sleeping at night.

A wide variety of similar studies have shown that the psychophysiological changes of PTSD are both extensive and enduring. Survivors do not have a normal baseline level of alert yet relaxed attention. Instead, they have an elevated baseline of arousal: Their bodies are always on the alert for danger. They also have an extreme startle response to unexpected stimuli as well as an intense reaction to specific stimuli associated with the traumatic event.[10]

Spiritual Loss

You may also experience a kind of spiritual wounding. N. Duncan Sinclair claims that PTSD is not even primarily a psychological or physiological disorder but, rather, "basically a spiritual dysfunction."[11] He describes ten spiritual attributes that are "grossly affected."[12] The spiritual losses may include: (1) loss of hope, (2) loss of intimacy, (3) loss of future, (4) loss of peacefulness, (5) loss of healing memory, (6) loss of spontaneity, (7) loss of wholeness, (8) loss of innocence, (9) loss of trust, and (10) loss of awe.

For you, physical and psychological losses may not be the most devastating loss. Inevitable questions may have risen up in your heart following your trauma. In her work on the biblical book of Jeremiah, Kathleen O'Connor describes the spiritual loss that follows trauma and disaster:

> Disasters mortally wound faith and trust. Confidence in God, the world, and other people can often dissolve in the wake of trauma, and such profound distrust can persist indefinitely. By itself, suffering does not bring an increase in love or meaning. Radical suffering corrodes trust, traditions, and institutions that anchored life firmly before the catastrophe. The once solid terrain of faith shatters, traditions collapse, and belief frays. Kai Erikson puts it this way: survivors of disaster "can be said to experience not only a changed sense of self and a changed way of relating to others but a changed worldview." Ways of thinking and acting that held people together with taken-for-granted certainty in the pre-disaster world

dissolve or are so sorely threatened as to no longer
support the world.[13]

Your spiritual loss may be amplified if you feel you have con-
tributed to the traumatic event. Your guilt may be crippling and
interfere with your relationship with God. Perhaps you were a
soldier called upon to kill others in a war. Or maybe you were the
driver in a horrific car accident caused by carelessness or alcohol
or maybe nothing at all. Kristin Vargas cites a 2009 journal article
by Brett Litz for giving credence to this very real spiritual loss.[14]
Experts and academics typically call this loss "moral injury."[15]

Your moral or spiritual injury may result in a wide range of trou-
bling feelings. First, rage—you may yearn for justice after such
deep harm or just be angry that your life turned out this way.
Second, fear—you may have learned too well that the world is dangerous. Third, distrust—who can be trusted now? Can even God
be trusted? Fourth, despair about the future—you may struggle
to care again about your life's mission and purpose. Your future
seems meaningless. Fifth, guilt—you may blame yourself for what
happened to you in an effort to regain your own agency. This can
be easier than accepting the reality that bad things sometimes
happen even though you did all of the right things. Or in some
cases, the survivor does carry a very real burden of guilt. Related
to this injury is the feeling of shame. Sixth, change in identity—you
may make the event the very center of your world. This is especially true if the event goes viral on social media. Seventh, lack
of meaning—you may struggle to give meaning to the traumatic
event. You may be asking, "Why?" The moral injury that you have
suffered is very real and can have a profound effect on your life.

Your Recovery Team

Just as real as your injury is the healing that God will provide as
he has promised. In fact, I expect that God will provide a whole
team of people to help you along the way. You might think of your

recovery from trauma as a team effort. The Lord will give you the opportunity to invite a variety of people onto your team to minister to your body, mind, and soul.

You may want to invite your medical doctor to be a part of your support team. Your doctor will know best how to help you with the physical effects of trauma.

You may also want to invite a Christian counselor with experience and training in trauma and PTSD to be a part of your support team. Many survivors would tell you that counseling was important in their recovery. After trauma, it may seem like an overwhelming task to find a counselor with whom you feel safe. You might ask your pastor or a trusted friend to help you locate a Christian counselor.

Currently, there are five prominent therapies that address trauma. They are (1) prolonged exposure therapy (PE), (2) cognitive processing therapy (CPT), (3) trauma-focused cognitive behavioral therapy (TF-CBT), (4) stress inoculation training (SIT), and (5) eye movement desensitization and reprocessing therapy (EMDR).[16]

Prolonged Exposure therapy, Cognitive Processing Therapy, and Trauma-Focused Cognitive Behavioral therapy are all therapeutic attempts to transform the survivor's trauma story. PE therapy has the simple goal of desensitizing the survivor to the traumatic memory. In PE, the survivor tells the story repeatedly until it is no longer shocking and no longer causes any sort of distress.

CPT and TF-CBT are similar in that they employ cognitive approaches to understanding the trauma story. In CPT, for example, survivors must write down an account of their trauma. Therapy sessions are then used to "challenge distorted beliefs about the event, self, and world through Socratic questioning and the use of a sequenced worksheet."[17]

Today, EMDR remains a popular and effective therapy for trauma. EMDR "conceptualizes insufficiently processed memories of traumatic or disturbing experiences as the primary basis for clinical pathology."[18] In EMDR therapy, the "practitioner directs the client to simultaneously move their eyes from side to side or employ some form of bilateral stimulation (e.g., alternating hand claps, alternating auditory tones), causing desensitization to the distressing traumatic memories, then reprocessing the memories so the associated cognitions become more adaptive."[19] In reviewing these five treatments, a peer-reviewed article concludes that these therapies all have high efficacy rates in lessening the symptoms of PTSD.[20]

These are not the only therapies available, but they are the ones most often used by counselors to treat trauma. As you think about which counselor you want to invite to join your support team, you might interview them. You can ask them about their familiarity with trauma. You can also ask what training they have and which therapy they would suggest for you. If the fit does not seem right or safe, continue your search. Like I said before, your pastor can help you here.

Finally, you may want to invite your pastor to be a key part of your recovery. Your medical doctor cares for your body. Your counselor helps with your mind. Most pastors are trained to be doctors of the soul. You have been wounded deeply, and there will be spiritual impacts. If you feel safe with your pastor, you very well may have found someone who can minister to your fear, guilt, or yearning for meaning. He may have even been your first call after your trauma. God has called him for just this moment.

This is also where this book fits. In fact, your pastor may have been the one who gave you this collection of letters. Deep as the Sea cannot replace the ministry of your church or your pastor, nor does it hope to do so. It also does not hope to replace the important place of counseling. Instead, I hope you use this book to minister to your wounded soul in the quiet moments during the week. This book is meant to be part of a multipronged effort to bring you back to life again. It is one resource among many that God will provide for you.

God's Psychological Word

I want to share with you why I would pick *Deep as the Sea* instead of a pensieve. In the Word of God, we hold in trembling hands the very power of God for salvation. We hold a Word of Life that not only determines what we believe but also speaks life into the whole person: reason, will, and emotion. Theologians have called the Word of God a psychological Word because it not only saves the sinner but also provides healing for the whole person.

Does that surprise you? Perhaps you have never thought about the Bible that way, but it's true. In the Word, we have the Spirit's tool that brings life where there is death. We have story after story after story of people undergoing trauma followed by God providing the hope of resurrection. The Word cleanses the emotions and impacts the heart. In the Word, we behold Jesus who suffered the trauma of the cross. In the Word, we have the same power that raised Jesus from the dead.

I am not saying that by placing the Bible on your lap, you will suddenly feel better. It will also not work to open your Bible app, press play, and then let your mind drift to other matters. The Word does not work like that. Martin Luther wrote,

> When we seriously ponder the Word, hear it, and put it to use, such is its power that it never departs without fruit. It always awakens new understanding, pleasure, and devotion, and it constantly creates clean hearts and minds. For this Word is not idle or dead, but effective and living.[21]

There is a delicate dance that takes place between the mind, body, and spirit in the human being.[22] What happens in the mind has tremendous impacts on the body and spirit and vice versa. For example, when a traumatic memory is triggered in the mind, the body physiologically responds with adrenaline and an elevated heart rate. In the spirit, fear is triggered. This interplay between mind, body, and spirit has massive implications for you the survivor. A letter to you, based on the promise of God's loving protection, will not just impact your spirit but also bring peace to your body and calmness to your mind. While my letter will target your spirit, it will inevitably impact your mind and body with healing power because of the dance.

Since the Word of God is a psychological Word, our search for cleansing and healing will start and end with the Word. It is for this reason that I have purposely chosen not to write a memoir. As powerful and inspiring as a memoir may be, *Deep as the Sea* will not enter this category. I am not writing my story. Instead, I want to wrap you up in Jesus' story. I want to move you from death to life, from the cross to the empty tomb.

The Letters and Their Order

This book is a compilation of letters. I write each letter to you on the basis of a Scripture passage, chosen with great care to speak into the specific spiritual needs of survivors. Each Scripture comes with its own unique power and perspective. You may wish to pause and reflect on each Scripture passage before you begin reading the body of the letter.

Each letter is a unit that can be read individually. However, the letters are knit together in a very intentional order. You are welcome to read *Deep as the Sea* in one sitting or read one letter at a time.

The letters are ordered according to the stages of healing that survivors of trauma may experience. (If you would like to read further about how recovery generally proceeds after trauma, you can turn to the epilogue.) The letters are grouped into three parts. Part One will speak into the spiritual needs of stage one of recovery: safety. Part Two will speak into the spiritual needs of stage two of recovery: remembrance and mourning. Part Three will speak into the spiritual needs of stage three of recovery: reconnection.

Part One
Safety

First
Letter

Deep as the Sea

*What can I say for you? With what can I compare
you, Daughter Jerusalem? To what can I liken
you, that I may comfort you, Virgin Daughter
Zion? Your wound is as deep as the sea. Who can
heal you?*

(Lamentations 2:13)

Dear Survivor,

More than a chapter goes by before he speaks to her. He could not see her or, perhaps, did not want to see her. I need to explain that comment a bit more. Let me give you my take on Lamentations, based on a book by Kathleen O'Connor, *Jeremiah, Pain and Promise*.

Lamentations chapters 1 and 2 have just two voices. The first is a male voice who serves as a kind of narrator. Perhaps it is the voice of Jeremiah the prophet, though we cannot be sure because he never identifies himself. This male voice seems distant for much of chapters 1 and 2. It is almost as if he is coldly and distantly narrating the destruction that he sees all around him. He is for much of these chapters nothing more and nothing less than a reporter. Jerusalem the golden, the city of God, has been leveled.

The second voice is a female voice. Cities in biblical times often were described and portrayed as women. Most Bible translations today indicate when the city-woman[23] is speaking in Lamentations by using quotation marks to set off her words. All of Lamentations chapter 1 goes by with the narrator simply observing and reporting the destruction of the city-woman, but the two do not converse. Meanwhile, the city-woman is begging anyone at all to see her— "Is it nothing to you, all you who pass by?" (Lamentations 1:12). Sadly, she finds no one to see her, not even the narrator. She feels all alone with her pain.

Then we get to our verse, Lamentations 2:13, and here we get a first: For the very first time, the narrator speaks to the woman. I am not sure what changed inside the narrator, if anything at all. I am not sure why he suddenly moved from seemingly being a distant observer, but something or someone moved him to become what the city-woman desperately needed: a compassionate witness. For the very first time, after almost two chapters, he sees her in all of her pain. For the very first time, he stops talking about her and speaks to her. Do you see the narrator pausing in front of the city-woman? Picture him sitting down in the dust and expressing that he sees her—and I mean, he truly sees her. Imagine him weeping with her and for her. Though he is truly seeing her, he doubts he can say or do anything for her. "What can I say for you?" he asks. The seemingly distant observer has been transformed into a compassionate witness.

I could be the narrator for a moment. I could even be a cold, distant narrator and recite the statistics about disaster, catastrophe, and trauma in this country today. I could tell you that 61% of men and 51% of women will suffer emotional trauma in their lives.[24] I could tell you that 20% of women will be sexually assaulted in their lifetime.[25] I could tell you that 7% to 8% of the US population will suffer from PTSD at some point in their lives.[26] I will be honest—rattling off statistics like these leaves me feeling cold and distant from you, Survivor. Numbers do not have faces and names and wounds. If there ever was a time when I could observe trauma in this way, that time is over.

I have a before and an after in my life. When I least expected it, I joined the 61% of men who have suffered trauma. I felt my own life slipping from my grasp. I said my last goodbyes. But then, I survived.

Then something I did not anticipate happened in the wake of my own trauma: People started telling me their stories. Person after person. Break-ins in the middle of the night. War stories in Iraq. Tragic car accidents. Childhood abuse. Rape. Husbands lost in the prime of life. Each time I heard a story, I was touched. The tears were always there, right below the surface. God was changing me. He was moving me from observer to compassionate witness. More than that, God was preparing me to write to you. He was leading me to ask the question our narrator in Lamentations asked by the power of the Spirit: "What can I say for you?"

"What can I say for you? . . . With what can I compare you? . . . Who can heal you?"

The answers seem to always come back in the negative. In my mind, the conversation goes something like this:

> I say, "What can I say for you?"
>
> She says, "Nothing. There is nothing you can say that will make it better."
>
> Then I try again: "With what can I compare you? How can I at least bring 'metaphorical restraint' to your pain?"[27]
>
> She responds, "You can't. There is no suffering like my suffering."
>
> Then I give it one last attempt: "Who can heal you?"
>
> She concludes, "No human can."
>
> I say, "Then your wound is as deep as the sea."

There is so much despair here, so much negativity, so much doubt that any word can bring hope or that anything can make it right. There is a part of me that agrees with that very sentiment. I have asked myself on so many occasions, "What can I say for you, the assault victim, or you, the grieving parent?" Part of me thinks, "Addressing trauma with words is dangerous, even the devil's plaything." I think of Job and the miserable comforters he had. Their words were nothing more than daggers, further wounding him. His friends antagonized him, blaming him for his pain, only making things worse. I know full well that the wrong word could do such spiritual damage. Part of me agrees, "There are no words for you."

And yet here in Lamentations 2:13, despair and hope are woven into the same poetic tapestry. The narrator gives the woman a new name, a resilient name. In fact, he repeatedly calls her the same name: Daughter.

Let me explain something here. Some survivors have had terrible fathers. For many people, fatherhood does not bring warm or happy thoughts. But the heavenly Father is tenderhearted and compassionate, pure in every respect, and never sinful or mean. God the Father is not just loving; he is love (1 John 4:8,16). He can't help it; it's his nature.

He could have called her "Harlot" or "Sinner" or "Woman with a Scarlet Letter" or other names she rightly deserved. After all, it was Jerusalem's stubborn unfaithfulness to the Lord and her spiritual adultery that led to her destruction. Instead, he draws near and says to her, "Daughter." He is drawing her into a restorative relationship with himself as her dear Father. What kind of father would leave his daughter in such ruin? What kind of father would see her in the ashes and look away? Not her heavenly Father. It was all true that the city-woman had rebelled against her Father, but the Father's love would seek her and find her and love her and cleanse her with the blood of Jesus. The Father would send his only Son to die for her and restore her to the family she had run away from. Even when she is in the dust, he names her "Daughter Zion." Hope has a heartbeat.

And you, Survivor, are no different. Whether your trauma can somehow be traced to something in you (as in the case of the city-woman) or the traumatic events were completely outside your influence, this is true for you: You also have been given this same resilient name in Christ:

"Son."

"Daughter."

Your eternal Father draws you in with the name he gives you through Christ. He will not leave you in your ruin. He cannot abandon you and still be your Father. He cannot forsake you and still be true to his great name. His love for you, which knows no bounds, and his power, which holds the world together, will hold you together too.

There is still more hope here. Even as the narrator asks his own despairing questions, he slowly begins to answer them. He doubts that he can compare her grief and loss to anything at all, but then he contradicts himself. He gives a comparison.

He says, "Your wound is as deep as the sea."

Even as he despairs of any comparison at all, he finds one. Your suffering is like the depths of the sea. Even as he is wondering if there is anyone who can heal the woman, he finds no one can, but he trusts that God can and that he will heal her.

It is as if he were saying, "I don't think there are any words for you, but I'm going to write three more chapters of this book. I don't think there is any comparison for your pain, but what about the depths of the ocean? I don't think any person can heal you, but I know someone who can: the Lord—Father, Son, and Holy Spirit."

There was a part of me that wanted to give up on this letter before I even began. I only have words. And yet I have *the* Word. I am convinced that no word from me will ever be sufficient. At the same time, I am equally convinced we have a true Word of Life in the Scriptures that speaks hope, forgiveness, purpose, and joy right back into our lives.

I am convinced that traumatic experiences cause wounds as deep as the sea itself. I am equally convinced that the love of God in Christ is deeper still. Jesus, who knew trauma intimately, suffered it just for us, to draw us to himself. I am convinced that while no human can heal trauma, God can. I am convinced that the Spirit, the true Comforter and Paraclete, can and will heal the deepest of spiritual wounds. I am right there with the narrator, despairing of myself and my own words but, at the same time, believing that God is true to his Word and that he not only can heal but will heal. He loves this city-woman and has a Word for her. He starts by sending to her a compassionate witness, someone to speak to her and for her.

Survivor, I see you and I have a Word for you.

Second Letter

Reclaiming Our Refuge

God is our refuge and strength, an ever-present help in trouble. Therefore we will not fear, though the earth give way and the mountains fall into the heart of the sea, though its waters roar and foam and the mountains quake with their surging.

There is a river whose streams make glad the city of God, the holy place where the Most High dwells. God is within her, she will not fall; God will help her at break of day. Nations are in uproar, kingdoms fall; he lifts his voice, the earth melts.

The Lord Almighty is with us; the God of Jacob is our fortress.

Come and see what the Lord has done, the desolations he has brought on the earth. He makes wars cease to the ends of the earth. He breaks the bow and shatters the spear; he burns the shields with fire. He says, "Be still, and know that I am God; I will be exalted among the nations, I will be exalted in the earth."

The Lord Almighty is with us; the God of Jacob is our fortress.

(Psalm 46:1-11)

Dear Survivor,

I wonder why the psalmist was meditating on such a nightmarish world. Just look at the first few verses. This is one apocalyptic, catastrophic disaster zone. In this world, previously safe places are not safe anymore. In this world, you may at any moment lose your life. This world is so unsafe that you cannot even trust the ground beneath your feet. The very earth is giving way, opening up as if to swallow you. That is not all. Off in the distance, you can see the mountains. They have stood for ages, impervious, proud, and immovable. Not anymore. The mountains are shaking. Their foundations are cracking. One by one, the mountains are falling into the very heart of the sea. Not even the mountains are safe! This is an absolute, apocalyptic nightmare. I wonder why. I wonder if it had anything to do with the memory of hundreds of thousands of bloodthirsty Assyrians outside the gates of Jerusalem. This may have been a very real scenario for the sons of Korah.

Adam—at least, that is what I will call him—could tell you what bent his imagination. He could remember a bright, sunny, almost cheery day driving down the road during his deployment in Iraq. He noticed a red sedan pass on the other side of the road. He smiled to himself—but not for long. Suddenly, his vehicle hit a land mine, flipping the whole caravan over. Years later, Adam is driving down a highway in the United States, and he feels anything but safe. He has just seen a red car flash by on the other side of the highway. In his mind, the memories flood back. His breathing becomes shallow. His heart is racing. He is reliving an apocalyptic nightmare in his imagination, and he knows exactly why.

This is what the APA calls a disorder. Over the years, the label doctors have given it has changed. For a while they called it hysteria.

Then it was called shell shock. Still later, doctors came up with a new and very odd collection of adjectives and nouns.[28] They started to call it post-traumatic stress disorder, or PTSD for short. Officially, it is a mental disorder under the category of fear in the diagnostic manual of the APA. Apparently, such an imagination is disconnected from reality and problematic for mental health. Such an imagination is disordered. That is what the APA says.

There is a part of me that bristles at such an idea. You know what I think is a more dangerous disorder? I will call it pre-traumatic naiveté disorder, or PTND for short. I see it in the young person cruising down the road, blasting his music. His left eye is on the road and his right eye is working on a text message. He does not care that he is going 70 mph in heavy traffic. I see it in the adrenaline junkie. She needs a rush, so she walks to the edge of the skyscraper because she knows she will never fall off. She is immortal. So tell me—whose imagination is closer to the truth? The one with PTSD or the one with PTND? The one who knows that disaster can strike at any time or the one who thinks he or she will never die?

Sometimes the mountains do fall into the heart of the sea. The veteran can tell you all about having a true enemy and what it means to count your days aright. The grieving family member can tell you about corporate greed and just how far it will go. The sexual assault victim can tell you about the sheer evil of lust and the craving for power. The accident survivor can tell you how a normal day with a normal itinerary can turn into total disaster in the blink of an eye. The Sons of Korah who penned this psalm likely could join in the chorus. They may have experienced hundreds of thousands of violent Assyrians sitting outside the gates of Jerusalem. Perhaps they heard the jeers of that army: "Soon, you will be eating your own filth." Disorder or not—disaster and trauma have a way of pushing the truths of evil, death, and sin deep into our hearts and our imaginations. To understand that disaster can happen at any moment is not a disorder. A true disorder is when your view of the world is disconnected from reality. It only becomes a disorder when you do not recognize another truth. If you see only danger everywhere and all the time, with no safe place for you, then you really do have a disordered imagination.

But you do have a safe place, a refuge that has never failed. When the ground beneath your feet is giving way, you have a refuge that is stronger still. When even the mountains are falling into the heart of the sea, you have a refuge that is more impervious than the mountains themselves. Who or what might that be? Psalm 46 tells us: "God is our refuge and strength, an ever-present help in trouble." I love that verse because it is honest about the fact that we will face trouble, big trouble. It is also honest about God: He is our refuge.

Let me tell you about a refuge. At its very core, a refuge is simply this: a safe place in the middle of the greatest danger. God is the ultimate refuge. Under his wings, we are completely safe. God is more trustworthy than the ground beneath our feet. He is more stable than the mountains on the horizon. God is our refuge.

We can see this in Jesus. When he walked the earth, dark spirits fled at his presence. When he spoke, demons begged for mercy. When the waves roared and foamed, when the disciples feared for their lives in the boat, Jesus stood up and said, "Be quiet." And the wind and waves sat down like an obedient dog and melted into nothing. "Who is this whom even the wind and the waves obey?" they asked. He is Jesus, our refuge.

I think about Jesus and his death. The earth shook when he gave himself in payment for all sin. The earth shook again when he rose, defeating death. It was as if the earth itself were shouting, "There is now something firmer and more stable than even the ground beneath your feet: the love and the power of Jesus, your refuge!" This same Jesus taught us to know our Father, who cares for every sparrow and numbers every hair on your head. God is our refuge and strength, an ever-present help in trouble.

"Therefore we will not fear." Let that sink into your heart for a second. Because God is our refuge, we can tell fear to take a hike. We need to take this gospel truth and push it so deep into our hearts that it informs everything else about us. We need to push it in so deep that the heart radiates its truth to the mind. When the red car drives by on the other side of the highway, we will not fear because God is our refuge. When we walk through the valley of the shadow of death, we will not fear because God is our refuge. When we get to that place or see that thing that caused us so much pain, we will not fear because God is our refuge. When we experience real danger, we will not fear because God is our refuge. We will take this truth and push it deep into our hearts. It will be like one of those cast-iron home radiators that warms every part of us. It will inform the disordered imagination and help to straighten up our disordered mind. We will hold the truth about evil and learn from it what we must, but we will hold even dearer the truth that even in our greatest trouble, God is our safe place.

After trauma, counselors and mental health professionals will almost certainly teach you new disciplines to help you when you get triggered by people or places or things or when you feel fear rising in your heart. They will probably talk to you about "grounding" yourself. There are several ways you can ground yourself in the present. They may teach you to rely on your senses. You might close your eyes and smell deeply, noticing the aromas in the air. You might open your eyes a little and notice the colors and details of the room. They may share with you the principles of mindfulness. All those techniques have a place in your recovery, but none of them can replace the power of Psalm 46. Your safety is found in God, who has never failed you.

Think about Adam again with me. His imagination was triggered when he saw the red car go by on the other side of the highway. What if Adam had pulled over on the side of the road and not only reminded himself that he was no longer in Iraq but also said to himself, "I thank you, God, my refuge, because in Iraq, you delivered me. When I needed you most, you were like a shield around me. That is the reason I am still here today. Your Word says that in you, I am safe"? Do you know what would happen if Adam did this? With time, with the help of the Spirit, with practice, his heart rate would slow. His mind would become calmer. His spirit would rejoice in God who saved him and was with him even then. God truly is our refuge.

I want you to imagine something with me. I want you to imagine a world where, on the outside, everything is falling. Mountains are falling into the heart of the sea. Nations and political kingdoms are falling into disorder and chaos. But in the middle of all this danger, there is also a city of refuge. I want you to imagine such a city. There is a river there flowing gently. Children are playing in the river. You can hear them laughing as they splash about. Adults love to sit next to the river early in the morning to meditate on the saving grace of their God. They are safe there because God is there. The people do not fear. They are singing, "The LORD Almighty is with us; the God of Jacob is our fortress" (Psalm 46:7).

Will you join me next to that stream? We are safe there. Healing will find us there in the presence of God, our refuge.

Part Two
Remembrance and Mourning

Third Letter

Prayer-Tears

The hearts of the people cry out to the Lord. You walls of Daughter Zion, let your tears flow like a river day and night; give yourself no relief, your eyes no rest.

Arise, cry out in the night, as the watches of the night begin; pour out your heart like water in the presence of the Lord. Lift up your hands to him for the lives of your children, who faint from hunger at every street corner.

"Look, Lord, and consider: Whom have you ever treated like this? Should women eat their offspring, the children they have cared for? Should priest and prophet be killed in the sanctuary of the Lord?

"Young and old lie together in the dust of the streets; my young men and young women have fallen by the sword. You have slain them in the day of your anger; you have slaughtered them without pity.

"As you summon to a feast day, so you summoned against me terrors on every side. In the day of the Lord's anger no one escaped or survived; those I cared for and reared my enemy has destroyed."

(Lamentations 2:18-22)

Dear Survivor,

The two voices—the compassionate witness and the city-woman—are back. They are talking, exchanging, and, most important, lamenting together.

The compassionate witness is now a compassionate counselor and gift giver. His first gift to the city-woman is the gift of prayer-tears. It may be his best gift. We call these prayer-tears a lament. From right there beside her in the dust, he tells her to cry out. He says it three different ways, poetically spilling water everywhere. He says, "Let your tears flow like a river," abundant in their lament to God, flowing to heaven itself. He says, "Cry out in the night," not even resting when others might. And again, "Pour out your heart like water in the presence of the LORD."

The city-woman does exactly as she is counseled. She takes up a lament with three simple parts. She opens herself up to God in complaint and petition. She addresses the Lord, her God and Savior. She brings accusations against the Lord—heavy accusations—and she petitions the Lord to see her pain. As she laments, the prayer-tears are accompanied by a desperate hope that God will hear her and see her. Her lament is the beginning of her hope.

Such a fountain of tears is striking when so much of the United States' culture wants you to live in denial about the way the world really is. Affluence, scientific achievement, and the rise of therapeutic culture all have conspired to lend the illusion of control to the US citizen. Trauma and suffering have been marginalized in our American consciousness. Too much of the church has participated in the dearth of tears, a desert devoid of them. Too many preachers push happiness and fulfillment, pushing laments to the side.

The loss of the lament is real and costly. You try to push away the pain or bury it. You believe that you can heal yourself through a combination of work and determination. If that does not succeed, you try to self-medicate the pain away. You might even tell yourself to change your attitude or suck it up, but none of it works. Your loss and grief will eventually catch up with you. If not right away, then when you least want them to appear. The tears will start, and they will not stop.

The biblical model for naming loss works differently. The book of Lamentations teaches you that it is good to bring your pain out into the open, into the very presence of God. You are encouraged to name every thing and person you have lost. You are encouraged to shed tears and leave your grief there in front of your heavenly Father, daring him to make wrong right. Patiently, he lets you accuse him if you must.

Let me be clear what this does not mean. It does not mean that lamenting is step number one of five neat and foolproof steps on your path to healing. It seems that much of secular culture and the Christian world would have you believe this. If you do the right things after trauma, you will not develop PTSD, or if you follow the right steps, then you will heal from PTSD quickly. At least, that is what they say. Scripture gives us a different approach to trauma—a gospel-centered and Christ-centered approach. Scripture, and its laments in particular, teaches healing as God's work. Lamenting does not ask you to change your attitude. It simply calls on you to cry out in all your pain and brokenness to God.

I want to give you even more reason to lament. Lamenting is biblical and Christ-like. We have a whole book in the Bible—Lamentations—filled with five haunting chapters of laments.

That is not all: 40% of the Psalms are laments.[29] Jesus used these laments throughout his life. Most famously, he put on his lips the words of Psalm 22:1, crying out, "My God, my God, why have you forsaken me?" (Matthew 27:46). Jesus' sufferings and death have given us not only a Savior from all guilt and shame before God but also one who can identify with our pain. In addition, the way he suffered and raised his laments to heaven also reinforces the power of a lament. By his blood, we can enter into the presence of God with all our hurts and complaints and know God accepts us as his forgiven children.

God transforms the believer through lamenting. A lament typically has five parts: (1) the address, (2) the complaint, (3) the request, (4) the promise, and finally (5) the expression of praise. Can you see how the Spirit moves a mourner to praise through these five elements? The lament wades deeply into loss by naming it honestly in God's presence. The lament then transforms the mourner into a worshiper through the gospel. Eugene Peterson says, "All true prayer pursued far enough will become praise.... It does not always get there easily.... But the end is always praise."[30]

Even psychology recognizes the power of grieving. Judith Herman's now classic book *Trauma and Recovery* names mourning as essential to recovery from trauma.[31] According to Herman, in the remembrance and mourning stage of recovery, survivors must name all they have lost. The only difference between Herman's mourning and the biblical lament is to whom the complaint and the mourning are addressed. A counselor can only witness tears; a lament is spoken to God.

And this is where tears become God's work. God has a threefold response to tears. First, he sees your tears (Psalm 56:8). Second, he cares about your tears (Psalm 34:18). Third, he promises one day to wipe them away (Revelation 7:17). How do we know this to be true? Because even in the deepest darkness, the cross of Jesus speaks to us of the love of God for us, and the empty tomb of Jesus speaks to us of his power to overcome even the greatest tear-producer, death. We have seen him respond to sorrows in the lives of others. Naomi comes to my mind in the biblical book of Ruth. The deaths of her husband and sons were so deep a loss that she tried to change her name. She wanted to be called Mara, meaning "bitter." The tears must have come regularly. God saw her tears and gave her a grandson. She kept her old name.

Let deep call out to deep.

Fourth Letter

Near Death, Near Resurrection

We do not want you to be uninformed, brothers and sisters, about the troubles we experienced in the province of Asia. We were under great pressure, far beyond our ability to endure, so that we despaired of life itself. Indeed, we felt we had received the sentence of death. But this happened that we might not rely on ourselves but on God, who raises the dead.

(2 Corinthians 1:8,9)

Dear Survivor,

Some people write about trauma from a safe distance. Doctors describe what happens to your body in the moment of trauma. The body automatically goes into survival mode and determines whether to fight, flee, or freeze. You become the purest kind of victim when you cannot run or even hope to fight. When you go into freeze mode, a switch flips in the brain and major systems in the body start shutting down. First, the stomach, kidneys, and intestines basically go offline. Next, the heart rate plunges, breathing slows, and the gut stops working. Sometimes the bladder empties. You can feel it in the pit of your stomach. "I am going to die," you tell yourself. Your body is trying to preserve as much energy as possible for the final struggle for life.[32] This is how scientists talk about it.

Hollywood, on the other hand, often attempts to romanticize the terror. It goes something like this: The character has just made what seems to be her very last attempt to escape. She realizes nothing she does or says matters now. She is totally powerless. A power much greater than herself is going to stamp her out. This is when the director cuts to the images running through her mind. She is remembering her life: running through flowery fields, getting a warm embrace from her father, playing hockey on a cold winter day with a smile on her face. Something like that. It seems they need to put life's slideshow into the victim's mind. That is how Hollywood wants to tell the trauma story.

The apostle Paul will not have either of these. He uses no medical jargon and definitely doesn't romanticize the near-death experience he shares. He just tells it like he felt it in his heart. He piles up words to speak the unspeakable and share the unshareable. He pictures a giant weight pressing down on him, saying he cannot endure it. He can do nothing to save himself. I want you to picture Paul in a garbage compactor. The compactor easily can crush flesh and bones. Not even the world's strongest man could leg press his way out. The garbage compactor's only job is to crush and destroy. A moment comes when the force is pressing against the lungs and head of the apostle. He announces his own death sentence: "This is my last moment. My life is over."

So many have pronounced such sentences in their own heads. Sexual assault victims. Genocide victims. Car accident victims. Soldiers in combat. Victims of gun violence. It feels like it is the end. Then suddenly and unexpectedly, the trash compactor stops, and they go on living.

Let us pause right there. Paul has experienced a trauma. He went through something that absolutely overwhelmed his own strength and coping mechanism. Then he went on living.

In the first moments after such a trauma, people go into shock. But this is not the hard part; that is yet to come. The hard part is learning to live with the memories. You somehow have to go back to living like before, but you can't—not yet. Do you know what you need in order to fully return to life? You need to know why. Isn't that the great trauma question? "Why? Why me? What was God doing when it happened to me?" Nobody can move on until he has the answer to those questions. Nobody can fully live again until she can tell her story.

I suppose Paul could have answered that question in different ways. He could have replayed it in his head over and over. He could have concluded the very worst: "God must be angry with me. His grace finally ran out. His promises of protection and angels are clearly bunk." He could have leapt to those devastating conclusions. He could have even begun to reconfigure his beliefs about God and the world through that one event, always reminding himself that he almost died. He could have become angry with

God, fearful of life, and even stopped living right there. He could have done that.

Many people do exactly that. They get stuck in the anger and fear. They come to the devasting conclusion that God abandoned them right when they needed him most. Some people will direct you down this path. I call them the mockers. They'll come at you with their insults right in the middle of your trauma: "And where was your God when that happened?" The mockers, the trolls, and even your own heart may begin to testify, "If there is a God, he surely wasn't there on that day!"

That is why I just love these verses in 2 Corinthians chapter 1. They speak so powerfully to someone who is living the post-traumatic life, looking for answers. The verses don't give the full answer to all the questions. However, they give the very best beginning of an answer. Listen to what the apostle says: "This happened that we might not rely on ourselves but on God, who raises the dead." Paul is not angry, and he is not on high alert for danger, because he knows God was there with him in the trauma with all his saving, resurrecting power.

Paul's trauma had brought home certain realities. The near-death experience had a continuing impact on his life. It taught him like never before just how weak he was. It taught him about death and his own mortality.

It spoke truths to Paul about the fallenness of this world and the depths of sin. But that was not all he learned. You see, Paul had come as close to death as you can without dying. The God of Jesus, who raises the dead, had brought him all the way from the brink of death back to life. The same God and Father who powerfully raised Jesus from the dead was also at work in Paul's life. For Paul, his trauma was not just a near-death experience; at the same time, it was also a near-resurrection experience. Right in the middle of his trauma, Paul experienced not less trust but more; not less safety but more; not less hope but so much more. In fact, Paul says he learned a lesson he hadn't learned well enough before. He now could trust in God more fully than ever. His God was the God of resurrection, the God of the cross and of the empty tomb.

While I was working on this letter, I happened to take in an episode of *60 Minutes* on a Sunday evening. I was transfixed by an interview with Chanel Miller. Some consider her to be the catalyst for the #MeToo movement, which seeks to address sexual abuse, harassment, and rape through personal testimony. Chanel experienced an awful sexual assault. As she told her story, you could see the sadness in her eyes. I kept wondering, "Where is God in her story? How does she get saved? How does her story end?" Later, the interviewer asked Chanel a profound question: "How did you carry on?" She said, "When I was reliving all of this, I thought—well, the same night the assault happened, a miracle also happened, which was that I was saved." She described how two Swedish students came along at just the right place and just the right time to save her from her attacker. The interviewer then said, "So they changed the story." And Chanel said with a huge smile, "They changed the story. They changed the entire trajectory of my life." I was moved to tears. Her story was not a story of abandonment by God but of a miracle and salvation.

Who has changed your story? Whom did God send into your life to bring you to life?

The apostle wants you to know—no, he needs you to know—that our God is the God of resurrection. He is the God of life. His very character is one of saving power. Just look at what he did for you! Through the saving death of Jesus, he brought you to himself. This God, who raises the dead, has not changed—not even a little bit. I am not asking you to deny the fact that we often suffer because of the brokenness of this world. We know that truth all too well. I am asking you to hold that truth together with gospel truth. The world is broken, and God has redeemed it. You have suffered a trauma, and God has brought you to safety. You nearly died, but you also have just nearly come back to life. It is not an either/or. It is a both/and.

It is right here in this truth that post-traumatic life begins. In order to truly live after trauma, we need to ground ourselves in the very character of God and in his Word. This God who raises the dead has not changed—not even a little bit. He is the God who saves. He is the God who raises the dead. He saved Chanel. He saved Paul. He saved me. Do you see what the great apostle is doing for us? He is giving us a new, biblical, Christ-centered perspective on our trauma and our lives. Why is it that you survived? Ask yourself that question. Really ask yourself that question. God saved you because of his great love for you. He saved you with his resurrecting power. Yes, you experienced something horrible, something words cannot describe. But you also experienced in real time the saving power of God from sheer evil. His saving power found you when you needed it most.

If you still need convincing, just ask Paul.

Fifth
Letter

What Can You Know?

"Can you fathom the mysteries of God? Can you probe the limits of the Almighty? They are higher than the heavens above—what can you do? They are deeper than the depths below—what can you know? Their measure is longer than the earth and wider than the sea.

"If he comes along and confines you in prison and convenes a court, who can oppose him? Surely he recognizes deceivers; and when he sees evil, does he not take note? But the witless can no more become wise than a wild donkey's colt can be born human."

(Job 11:7-12)

Dear Survivor,

Zophar is a jerk. I mean it. Have you considered what Zophar, Job's supposed friend, has just said to him? Open your Bible and read the first six verses of Job chapter 11. Zophar had shown up shortly after the funeral of Job's ten children and told him, "You deserved this loss because of your sins." Zophar gets even crueler than that. He says, "Job, your sins deserve worse than what you have gotten. God has even forgotten some of your sin." All three of Job's friends say awful things, but Eliphaz, the first friend to speak, says it with honey mixed in. Bildad, the second to address Job, coats his attack with nice plastered on his face. But Zophar is on a whole other level. He is a total jerk.

The last thing I want to do is tell you he is right, but I must. Zophar may be a jerk, he may be mean, but he is also right—at least partly. He is poetically and artfully right. The mystery of God is higher than the heavens. The purposes of God are deeper than deep. The measure of God's plans is longer than the earth and wider than the sea. Since God's ways are higher than ours and his thoughts deeper than ours, what can you really know about what God is doing? How can you claim with any kind of certainty what God is doing through disaster or crisis or trauma? You cannot know any more than you can climb up to heaven yourself. You just cannot know. Zophar is right.

So is Isaiah. He is the prophet who recorded God saying, "As the heavens are higher than the earth, so are my ways higher than your ways and my thoughts than your thoughts" (Isaiah 55:9).

The apostle Paul is right too. He brims over in doxology when contemplating such mystery: "Oh, the depth of the riches of the wisdom and knowledge of God! How unsearchable his judgments, and his paths beyond tracing out!" (Romans 11:33). Isaiah, Paul, and Zophar all teach the same beautiful truth: Trying to understand God's ways or trace his logic is like trying to measure the ocean with a tablespoon. It cannot be done. God is a hidden God. As much as it pains me to say it, Zophar is right.

Zophar is also wrong. Very wrong. Not about the fact that God is inscrutable and his ways mysterious and his thoughts higher than the heavens. Zophar is wrong about what he says next. He is so wrong that it is ironic. He has just told Job he cannot possibly know the mind of God, but then he tries explaining to Job exactly why God is making him suffer. He tells Job God has already judged his sin and marked him as a deceiver. He wraps everything up by telling Job he has the same chance at becoming wise as a donkey has of giving birth to a human being. But Zophar is wrong to pretend to know Job's why. He is wrong to think he has climbed up into heaven itself and can tell Job why his kids died and why he has to suffer in the way he is. Zophar is the fool. Zophar is the witless one.

Survivor, do not be Zophar. Do not claim to know why. You will then avoid lurching from one guess to the next as your life's story continues to unravel. It is enough to know that God has a purpose for you, one that is deeper and wider than the sea.

In his book *Where Is God When It Hurts?* Philip Yancey lays out just how uncertain all the certainty can be.[33] He tells a true story of some "Zophars" and a lady named Claudia, who described all the visitors she got in the hospital as she was suffering from cancer. A deacon came by and told her she had sinned and that God was warning and punishing her. A fellow church member told her she just needed to claim victory over her Hodgkin's disease, implying she was sick because she did not trust God enough. Then her pastor rolled in and told her she should be thankful for the disease because God was rewarding her faith: she was getting to be an example of strength and integrity. Claudia was left angry and confused by the contradictory messages. Yet it is not just Claudia hearing these kinds of messages. There are Zophars old and new.

We may not even realize when we are pulling a Zophar ourselves. We construct neat little explanations for things we cannot understand so that we feel more secure. This is how we cope with incomprehensibility. We lay a neat little theory over what is incomprehensible and tell ourselves it is true, and then we can at least have that much certainty. We pull a Zophar. Do you know why Zophar had to believe Job was suffering for his sin? Then he could be certain. He could be certain that what happened to Job would not happen to him.

So "what can you know?" (Job 11:8). With that question, Zophar wanted to humble Job, to put Job in his place, to tell Job he didn't have the wisdom to understand why God does what he does. But stay with Zophar's question a little bit longer. We cannot know God's hidden counsels or why he brought about tragedy in our lives or discover his character through crisis. Those things are hidden from us.

So what can you know? Stay with that question long enough, and you will hear truths that never came out of Zophar's mouth but instead came out of Job's with absolute conviction. These are truths that do not paint God as a capricious monster or guess at the provisional, but truths that are bedrock for the toughest moments. Triumphant truths. Truths like that exploded out of Job's heart even as he plunged into the depths of despair. He said, "I know that my redeemer lives" (Job 19:25). This was the conviction of Job's heart and his confident testimony. He could see Jesus coming! By faith, Job could see Jesus, who suffered and died. That death seems so unjust, so senseless, so meaningless on the face of it. But it was not. The Son of God suffered not only in solidarity with us but also in our place for all sin. Then God gave Jesus the victory over sin and death. Job foresaw this, at least in part. He could not explain his own suffering and loss, but he did know one thing for certain: He had a living Redeemer. He had someone who could redeem us—buy us back—from sin and death, someone who could give meaning to our worst tragedies and losses. That is what Job knew, and that was enough for him for the moment. That is ultimately the truth we can hold to in trauma and crisis and disaster. We cannot know God's purposes, but we can know our Redeemer Jesus.

Now I could tell you that, in theological terms, we are talking about the hiddenness of God and the revelation of God in Jesus Christ. I could spit out theological axioms like "Let our hidden God remain hidden where he wants to remain hidden." I could offer answers for those great theological and philosophical questions like "Why do bad things happen to good people?"

I could further give you all kinds of philosophical terms like the problem of evil and the various theodicies that have been proposed over the years. I could answer for you one of the great philosophical questions: How can evil coexist with a good God?

But our questions are not primarily theological or philosophical. They are emotional and personal and primal. They sound more like this: "Why did my child die?" "Why did God allow me to be raped that night?" "Why did I survive, but my friend, who is far more talented, die?"

And the best answer to those questions may be: Only God knows. I will not venture a guess to know his mind. But I do know this: I know that God's wisdom reaches the heavens. I know that his purposes are as wide as the ocean. I know also that through Jesus, God knows suffering. And he knows victory over suffering, sin, and death. And best of all, I know that the love of God in Christ Jesus is high and wide and deep and long, and nothing can separate us from it! That is what I know, and that is enough.

I am not God. I will not pretend to be, but I do know something. You certainly do not need my guesses or speculations. You also may not need a theological treatise or a philosophical debate. Instead, you need to know that God's ways are, and always will be, far above our ways. Yet because of his vast and mysterious plan, sinners are saved. Our God is beyond measure—wider than the ocean, higher than the heavens, deeper than the sea—and so is his love in Christ. To be known by him and named by him and loved by him is enough. More than enough.

Postscript

I thought about it more. You may actually want to get into the theological and the philosophical ever so briefly. Keep reading if you might find a little detour like that helpful for your heart. If so, buckle up. We are going to go deep and fast.

A Theological Response to the Problem of Evil

In 1518 at the beginning of the Lutheran Reformation, Martin Luther wrote a set of theses (theological propositions) for debate at a meeting in Heidelberg, Germany. The meeting came to be known as the Heidelberg Disputation. Theses 18-20 are worth considering as we seek to know what is hidden and what meaning can be made of trauma and disaster. In these theses, Luther lays out a theology of the cross as opposed to a theology of glory.

18. That person does not deserve to be called a theologian who looks upon the invisible things of God as though they were clearly perceptible in those things which have actually happened (Rom. 1:20).
19. He deserves to be called a theologian, however, who comprehends the visible and manifest things of God seen through suffering and the cross.
20. A theology of glory calls evil good and good evil. A theology of the cross calls the thing what it actually is.[34]

With these three theses, Luther dramatically brought out what Scripture has always taught: God saved us through the trauma of Jesus on his cross. Human wisdom calls the cross foolish and offensive. God calls it saving. Luther states that a theologian of the cross will be able to name what is both good and evil in life through the lens of the cross, while a theologian of glory will often confuse them, calling evil good and good evil. Stated another way, the theologian of glory looks for God to be visible in life's triumphs and victories, while the theologian of the cross can see God working in defeat and shame.

Dear Survivor, consider this as it relates to your trauma. True evil and true good can never be taken at face value but must be discerned with the Word and the Spirit. Evil and good can only be known as they relate to the cross of Jesus. Does the traumatizing event we experienced separate us from God and his love? Then it is evil. Does it bring us closer to God? Then how could it be evil?

Because a thing's true nature can only be comprehended through suffering and the cross, Luther taught that God hides himself. He cannot be found out by looking at events in our lives or by the memory of our experiences. He can only be found where he wants to be found, and he wants to be found suffering on a cross in Jesus Christ for our sins. This is where the genuine God is revealed to us in his Word. Luther often spoke along these lines:

> The Diatribe [of Erasmus], however, deceives herself in her ignorance by not making any distinction between God preached and God hidden (*Deus absconditus*), that is, between the Word of God and God Himself. God does many things that he does not disclose to us in his word; he also wills many things which he does not disclose himself as willing in his word.[35]
>
> God also does not manifest himself except through his works and word because the meaning of these is understood in some measure. Whatever else belongs essentially to the Divinity cannot be grasped and understood.[36]

John Schaller makes the same point in his stunning essay "The Hidden God":

> Isaiah once gave expression to the same realization—and in the middle of a sermon in which he was proclaiming a wonderful truth from the lips of God, a truth which he could have learned only through God's revelation. Under the powerful influence of the truths God was unveiling to him, Isaiah addressed God directly with the words: "Verily, Thou art a God that hidest Thyself, O God of Israel, the Savior!" (Is 45:15). The same God who through prophets and apostles gave us revelations concerning His being and His will; the same God who in Jesus Christ Himself became man and as the God-man draws ever so close to us—this revealed God remains at the same time *a hidden God!*[37]

A Philosophical Response to the Problem of Evil: Theodicy

Theodicy is a philosophical defense of God in the face of evil's existence. It seeks to answer this basic question: If God is good, how did evil come to be? In the essay "Christian Apologetics in a Post/Modern Context," Samuel Degner outlines several possible theodicies. The first comes from St. Augustine.

1. God created the universe and everything was good.
2. Some of God's creation had the good gift of free will.
3. Some freely chose to turn from God's goodness.
4. This brought evil into the universe.
5. Evil is not a thing; it is a deprivation of good.
6. God will rectify evil when he judges the world.[38]

This is one possible explanation for the existence of evil next to a good God.

Alvin Plantinga offers another approach:

> A world containing creatures who are significantly free (and freely perform more good than evil actions) is more valuable, all else being equal, than a world containing no free creatures at all. Now God can create free creatures, but he can't cause or determine them to do only what is right. For if he does so, then they aren't significantly free after all, they do not do what is right freely. To create creatures capable of moral good, therefore, he must create creatures capable of moral evil; and he can't give these creatures the freedom to perform evil and at the same time prevent them from doing so. As it turns out, sadly enough, some of the free creatures God created went wrong in the exercise of their freedom; this is the source of moral evil. The fact that free creatures sometimes go wrong, however, neither counts against God's omnipotence nor against his goodness; for he could have forestalled the occurrence of moral evil only by removing the possibility of moral good.[39]

One more explanation of the problem of evil is what is sometimes called the soul-making theory. This theodicy is outlined in different ways by different philosophers, but the basic version says that God uses trauma and hardship to refine moral character and to drive the sufferer to see his or her need for God.

Perhaps the best approach is what Jeff Mallinson called a narration of evil, which "does not explain away or try to show how particular instances of evil produce some greater good." Instead, it starts with what we know about the God who suffered on the cross for all sin to give us an eternal future without evil. We may not be able to understand the why of evil or how God makes it serve his purposes, but we can settle our hearts on the character of

God and his loving intentions. Ultimately, "Christ is God's answer to the problem of evil."[40]

Sixth
Letter

The Glory in His Shame

*Adam and his wife were both naked, and they felt
no shame.*

*Then the eyes of both of them were opened,
and they realized they were naked; so they sewed
fig leaves together and made coverings
for themselves.*

*The LORD God made garments of skin for Adam
and his wife and clothed them.*

(Genesis 2:25; 3:7,21)

Dear Survivor,

I am always struck at how Moses tells our origin stories, especially when he tells the origin story of sin. Even though I have read the story about the fall into sin hundreds, maybe even thousands, of times, I am almost always surprised. Honestly, I almost always expect Adam and Eve to be overcome with fear. The Lord God had told them that if they ate the forbidden fruit, then they would most certainly die. You would think they would be frozen in terror after eating the fruit, like two people who had just drunk poison. Or you would think they would expect the Lord God to turn into their executioner and they, in turn, would be turned into fearful people, begging for mercy. Yet that is not the scene that unfolds in the garden. It is not the expected fear or guilt or even sadness. Something else is far more pressing.

Instead, it is spiritual shame that overwhelmed them in that moment. Everything seemed to happen in slow motion. First, their eyes were opened. Adam looked at his wife and saw sin—he had seen her do it. Eve looked at her husband and saw sin—she had seen him do it. They were both eyewitnesses to their mutual crime.

Next, they realized they were naked. They felt exposed not only physically but also spiritually. It was not as if their perfect bodies had suddenly developed blemishes. This was not the very first case of body-shaming. It was soul shame. Their tender souls no longer felt safe even with their own best friend and spouse.

Finally, they started sewing together fig leaves. Their shame was so deep and so desperate that they may have first used their hands to cover themselves. They were smart enough, however, to realize that wouldn't work for long. So they must have run to the nearest tree, grabbing for anything that might cover their incredible shame.

They settled on fig leaves. Can you imagine their new outfit haphazardly sewn together with twigs and vines and fig leaves? Can you imagine the "fig leaf fails"? It must have been the most ridiculous scene in the short history of the world, but what else could they do? Seriously, they felt compelled to conceal their shame somehow.

So do we. Once, when I had fallen deeply asleep at home, my three little girls got it into their minds to paint my toenails hot pink. They snuck over quietly and painted away. They must have had the time of their lives, giggling while they painted away. When they finished their brilliant, artistic work, they woke me up. We laughed about it, and I figured it would wear off eventually. Later that week, I showed up at my gym to work out. I went into the locker room to change my shoes, and then I remembered: I have hot pink toenails! You should have seen the looks from that diverse group of New Yorkers. A part of me wanted to run and hide or at least explain to them how it had happened that my toes shone so brightly. You should have seen me trying to cover my hot pink toes. I thought, "This is shame." This is what Adam and Eve felt, but my shame was nowhere near theirs—or the shame one may feel after trauma.

Sometimes shame comes because of your own guilt, but sometimes it is inflicted on you. Sometimes it is painted on by someone else. This is the kind of shame that you, Survivor, may carry in your heart. Shame can be suffered. Elie Wiesel, himself a Holocaust survivor and prolific writer, wrote so poetically, "Shame tortures not the executioners but their victims. The greatest shame is to have been chosen."[41] And he is right. Just ask any survivor of injustice or abuse or sexual assault. When something or someone makes you feel small and weak, like something to be used and then thrown away, shame floods the heart. Intense shame. You become the piece of garbage their actions or words named you.

And this shame has power over us. It runs deep, in some cases deeper than fear or guilt or sadness. Harold Senkbeil writes, "Guilt has to do with behavior, while shame is a matter of identity."[42] Diane

Langberg said, "Shame is not just a feeling, though it is profoundly that. Shame is a sense of self . . . as defective, empty, worthless, and trashed."[43] Shame goes to the heart of who we are—of who Adam and Eve had become.

Shame has such power that it can become a kind of script or mantra. If you pay close enough attention to your spiritual inner life, you might be able to hear the voice of shame constantly whispering. You lose in a game, and your immediate self-accusation is "I am such a loser." No one hears you say it, but you believe it all the same. You have another failed relationship, and you immediately know why: "How could anyone possibly love me? I am ugly and broken." You make a mistake at work and are immediately defeated: "I am just so incompetent." These feelings and beliefs can be so entrenched that you cannot think any other way about yourself. It all comes from shame. Shame has thrust its way into your life; it was inflicted on you, or you may have done something morally wrong and inflicted it on yourself.

So you grab whatever is nearest, maybe a feather or fig leaves, and hope for the best because you have to cover up this shame. Sometimes the best fig leaf is to attack others, to protest too much, to shove off responsibility. Sometimes the best fig leaf is to run away from the shame, to dive deep into drugs, alcohol, sex, work, or other distractions. Sometimes the best fig leaf is to freeze up and pretend it never happened. But fig leaves cannot cover shame in any lasting way. They fall apart and leave you naked again. Remember, Survivor, your eyes are open now.

God's eyes are always open too. Having seen the naked, shame-filled, fig leaf-covered couple, he does not become the executioner we might have expected. Instead, the Lord God becomes a tailor for them. Moses tells us, "The LORD God made garments of skin for Adam and his wife and clothed them" (Genesis 3:21). The Lord simply could not set aside his love for Adam and Eve. His love was so deep that it seems he ruined part of his creation for them. Did he perhaps take rabbits, a bear, or a cow and make leather? Moses does not tell us. He does not tell us how the One who had created all life may have suddenly ended a life for Adam and Eve. Moses simply reports that the Creator sewed garments of skin. His fatherly heart did everything necessary to help them.

God would go still further. He would send Jesus to battle Satan, not in paradise but half-starved in the desert. He would send Jesus to live in perfect righteousness and innocence. He would send Jesus not to be skinned but crucified—to shed the innocent blood that would be the perfect covering for sin and shame. He would send Jesus to be the second Adam, to undo the damage done by the first Adam. Just as Adam was the genesis of your sin, your death, and your shame before God, Jesus is the genesis of your forgiveness, your life, and your glory. God never wanted to become your executioner. He never planned to be the one to lead you down the hall to death row and sit you in the electric chair. God's goal was always to be a Savior for you. His goal was to make you garments as holy and good and righteous as Jesus himself.

Sometimes my daughters do fashion shows for me. They always beg for my attention. When they have it, they come down our staircase with a set of clothes on. Their heads are held high. They have smiles on their faces, and they know they are loved. They say, "Daddy, look!" And I say, "Wow! Just wow!" And in that moment, shame has no place, only glory in what God has done for these little ones he has loved.

You see, your shame covered by Jesus and his righteousness means glory for you. How can you shrink into the darkness when you are covered with such priceless robes? It means more than just glory. It means you can shut the sewing machine down. Why do you need to lash out when your shame is so wholly covered? Why do you need to drown yourself in self-medication when you are so wholly loved and adored? Why do you need to stay frozen in life when the love of God in Christ has so warmed your heart? And those scripts that bring such self-condemnation into your heart—why would you mutter such lies about yourself? How can you ever say in your own heart, "I cannot be loved" or "I am beyond help" or "I am ugly" when you have become the very bride of Christ? Shame covered by Jesus cries out, "Glory to God!" And that is what you are. The shame he endured for you has become your glory.

You are not the shame that comes from past mistakes, and you are not the shame someone inflicted on you. Through Jesus, you are the glory of God.

Seventh
Letter

Survivor's Guilt

Then he showed me Joshua the high priest standing before the angel of the LORD, and Satan standing at his right side to accuse him. The LORD said to Satan, "The LORD rebuke you, Satan! The LORD, who has chosen Jerusalem, rebuke you! Is not this man a burning stick snatched from the fire?"

(Zechariah 3:1,2)

Dear Survivor,

Guilt runs both wide and deep. There are as many versions of guilt as there are shades of blue. There is the parental version, the student version, the spousal version, the child of God version, the employee version. I could go on. Guilt runs wide. It also runs deep. Survivor's guilt is deep guilt.

The title of a video caught my eye: "A Son Grapples with Guilt: Did He Give His Father the Coronavirus?"[44] Gianni worked for a bike-sharing service in Milan, Italy. He continued to go to work until he could not anymore. He felt faint and hardly had any strength. His father, Antonio, lived with him and also got sick. When they both were too weak to continue on alone, the same ambulance carried them both away. Gianni survived the coronavirus, but Antonio did not. After Gianni recovered, he walked into his father's now empty room. Fifteen days had passed since the ambulance arrived. All his dad's things were still there. The guilt hung in the air as thick as the memories. Gianni survived COVID-19, but now he was struggling with the guilt. Did he make his own father sick? And how dare he survive when his father didn't? Survivor's guilt runs deep and accusingly.

So many Scriptures can powerfully minister to this type of guilt. I looked at many possibilities for this letter, but I kept coming back to these verses in Zechariah chapter 3. Of all the verses in the Bible, I think these two speak most powerfully into survivor's guilt with one specific empowering action: They call on us to rebuke it in Jesus' name. In this letter, I want to tell you why and how to carry this out.

I need you to really see this with me. Joshua, the high priest, is standing before the Angel of the Lord (that's Jesus). Joshua represents the entire community of Israel, which has returned after

70 years of exile in Babylon. Standing at Joshua's right is Satan. From this perfect pulpit, he whispers straight into Joshua's soul. We are not told what accusations Satan was pushing into Joshua's heart before the Lord, but we can guess. Maybe it sounded like this: "Joshua, you are a failure! You are such a failure before the Lord. It's no surprise though. You come from a long line of corrupt priests, and you fit the pattern. Joshua, you are a failure! You spent a long time in Babylon, and the wickedness of that pagan society clings to you. What makes you think you can minister in this new temple? Joshua, Joshua, you survived the exile, but what use are you to the Lord?" There Joshua stood, with all of his exilic guilt, being used by Satan for target practice in the presence of the Angel of the Lord.

Guilt has a constant companion, a helper. Satan loves to push guilt into your heart. He makes your ear his pulpit. At times, he is eloquent and convicting. "At that moment, you made the wrong choice. If you had only done things differently, if you had just risen to the moment, it would not have happened. But you did not rise to the moment; you did not make the right choice. Now you have to live with the guilt. Every day. Every moment." This is what he whispers into your heart, changing the words just enough to make the accusations more specific to your trauma. Can you hear him working to keep you in guilt?

Do you see Joshua standing there paralyzed? He is frozen. He may be reliving his poor decisions—maybe one in particular.

When Joshua first got back to Jerusalem from exile in Babylon, he and the other returning people rebuilt the altar to the Lord. Soon they began rebuilding the temple. But the building project slowed down and eventually stopped. For 17 years, the Lord's house remained untouched, even neglected under rain and the other elements, while the people built houses for themselves. As the high priest, Joshua may have participated in this neglect. Now he is standing in front of God with Satan standing there too, bringing up Joshua's sins.

In J. R. R. Tolkien's *The Lord of the Rings,* a man named Wormtongue has become the advisor to Théoden, King of Rohan. Wormtongue, with his pale and ugly face, sits next to Théoden, whispering lies and guilt into the king's ear. Théoden becomes a puppet of Wormtongue. The advisor's influence is so powerful that the king begins to age quickly, losing his strength and courage for his people and kingdom. Théoden, like Joshua, becomes stuck in the paralyzing power of guilt.

Satan uses survivor's guilt to paralyze. It is a little bit like a spider bite or a snakebite: He poisons you with it, and then he just leaves to devour you later.

If it had been up to Joshua, he would have stayed in his vegetative state, but it was not up to him. It was up to Jesus because he saw what was going on, and so Jesus, the Angel of the Lord, does something very out of character. He gets really, really mad. He becomes enraged. He boils over. I say this is uncharacteristic because normally our Lord does not react quickly with incredible anger. Normally, he is slow to anger. In fact, we have an Old Testament creed that says this very thing about the Lord. The Lord is slow to anger and abounding in love and faithfulness, except when he deals with satanic guilt. I mean, look at what he does here: He is not slow to anger. He is quick to anger. He is not abounding in love for Satan. Instead, he drives Satan back. The Lord says to him, "The LORD rebuke you, Satan! The LORD, who has chosen Jerusalem, rebuke you! Is not this man a burning stick snatched from the fire?" (Zechariah 3:2). You can almost sense the emotion of the scene because of the repetition of the rebuke. He does not bring the rebuke just once but twice: "The LORD rebuke you! The LORD rebuke you!" And all in a moment, the Lord rises up and performs an exorcism on the right ear of Joshua. The Lord has put an end to both the source and the power of guilt on Joshua. He will not listen to the accusations, not even one word.

Let me be clear: I'm not talking about presumed guilt, the kind that sneaks in even though you've done nothing to cause your traumatic event. Or the kind that threatens to overwhelm you because you survived but others didn't. Even still, when Satan accuses us, he will scramble it all together with our moral guilt. In this sense, he is not totally wrong. That is why his lies always resonate with us. They can be partly, even mostly, true.

Whether the moral kind or not, you carry feelings of guilt. You know it. Satan knows it. Jesus knows it. Like Joshua, we are burning sticks snatched from the fire, but Jesus is not listening to accusations. Instead, he sends Satan packing with a rebuke.

Even when it comes to our moral guilt, the kind that comes from breaking God's laws, Jesus doesn't ignore it. He had a plan for dealing with those paralyzing accusations: "I will take on human flesh, take on the whole world's load of guilt, and die in the place of Joshua and all the rest of humankind. My death will satisfy my Father's wrath against sin. Then Satan's accusations will no longer be valid. He will be thrown out of God's courtroom every time. Who can ever successfully accuse my redeemed people if I take their place?" And then Jesus did just that. He died, and then he rose, for you and for me. Guilt, both real and imagined, is gone from God's courtroom, and our Savior sends Satan packing with a rebuke. Satan's law license has been revoked by the blood of Jesus.

A Veterans Day article in *The New York Times Magazine* movingly described one warrior's struggle with survivor's guilt. The title said everything: "I Watched Friends Die in Afghanistan. The Guilt Nearly Killed Me."[45] He talked about the years spent reliving those critical moments when his friends died in battle. Could he have done more? Should he have done more? Should he even have survived? Was the guilt he felt real? Was it self-imposed? The answers never seemed to come, and the guilt consumed him. Satan had him right where he wanted him for a long time. But what if this veteran had found rest in knowing that Jesus had pardoned him for whatever guilt was on his record? What if he had simply let Jesus' blood cover him years earlier? The cross of Jesus sets us free from guilty questions and recriminations. It washes over us like a cleansing, unending flood.

Do you know what this means? Rise up today in Jesus' name. Look Satan in the face and tell him, "If I messed up in any way, my Savior has paid for my sin. In fact, my Jesus has the answer for every accusation of guilt, real or imagined. The Lord Jesus has closed the heavenly courtroom and locked it because his decision has already been made. In Jesus' name, I am not guilty of what you say. 'There is now no condemnation for those who are in Christ Jesus' (Romans 8:1). Your accusations have no place in my life. I am forgiven. I am a survivor free from guilt. The Lord rebuke you, Satan! The Lord rebuke you!"

Survivor, tomorrow is a new day and Jesus has loved you to death.

Eighth Letter

One Little Word

"Can you pull in Leviathan with a fishhook or
tie down its tongue with a rope? Can you put
a cord through its nose or pierce its jaw with a
hook? Will it keep begging you for mercy? Will
it speak to you with gentle words? Will it make
an agreement with you for you to take it as your
slave for life? Can you make a pet of it like a
bird or put it on a leash for the young women
in your house? Will traders barter for it? Will
they divide it up among the merchants? Can
you fill its hide with harpoons or its head with
fishing spears? If you lay a hand on it, you will
remember the struggle and never do it again! Any
hope of subduing it is false; the mere sight of it is
overpowering. No one is fierce enough to rouse it.
Who then is able to stand against me? Who has
a claim against me that I must pay? Everything
under heaven belongs to me.

"Nothing on earth is its equal—a creature without
fear. It looks down on all that are haughty; it is
king over all that are proud."

(Job 41:1-11,33,34)

Dear Survivor,

There is real genius in Martin Luther's great hymn "A Mighty Fortress Is Our God."[46] Christians have been singing it since the 1500s. Even Roman Catholics now sing this hymn of the Lutheran Reformation! The church never seems to tire of it. There is also real depth to this hymn, which we may fail to recognize, like the last line of the first stanza: "On earth is not his equal." With that little line, Luther did two things. First, he brought into our hymn Job's Leviathan. Luther used the same German word *(seinsgleichen)* in both the hymn and his translation of Job 41:33: "Nothing on earth is its equal." Second, he dispensed with the zoology.[47]

It is easy to get distracted by the zoology of Job chapter 41. Do you wonder too about this beast's identity? This is one incredible creature—the one without equal. I too get caught up in the details, like its body armor. I mean, this body armor sounds better than any military body armor ever developed. The rows of shields across its body are so tight that "no air can pass between" (Job 41:16). Then there is its breath. It is not that Leviathan had bad breath but that it actually breathed fire! "Flames stream from its mouth" (Job 41:19). Fighting it is futile. Javelins bounce off its hide. "Iron it treats like straw and bronze like rotten wood" (Job 41:27). I can imagine modern-day bullets glancing off harmlessly. And Leviathan looks like an ocean liner as "it leaves a glistening wake behind it" (Job 41:32). A creature like that truly has no equal on earth.

Now this is where people start going crazy with the zoology. They want to pin down exactly what Leviathan is or was. Some people think God created his own version of the movie *How to Train Your Dragon.* They charge that God has started to live in a fantasy world of wizards and dragons and knights. Others maintain that Leviathan is not fantasy at all but a real part of creation. They specify that Leviathan is a crocodile and not an alligator because, they say, alligators are gentle and only attack when necessary. Crocodiles, however, are just plain violent and will take down whatever they can, even if they are not hungry. Still others are confident that here we have a dinosaur sighting in the Bible. Job chapter 41 can spur a Loch Ness Monster kind of obsession, and attempting zoological identification is as far as people get. George Bernard Shaw famously complained that Job wanted to know why he was suffering, but all God could do was talk about snowflakes and crocodiles.[48]

But I think Luther will not have it. I think that for Luther, no other creature could rightly be without equal on earth except the old evil foe. Can you think of a more powerful creature? Luther follows Moses, who does not get too caught up on the identity of the serpent in the garden. Moses already knew that a talking snake just had to be Satan.

Luther follows Isaiah, who called Leviathan a serpent. I think he also saw the apostle John as describing Leviathan in such detail that he eventually penned, "The great dragon was hurled down— that ancient serpent called the devil, or Satan" (Revelation 12:9). For Luther, applying Job's description of Leviathan to Satan was a simple matter. We have good reasons to do the same, even though other good Christian people may see it differently. The creature that has no equal on earth, the creature that can overpower us just with a mere look, is the great violator, the great perpetrator, the old evil foe, Satan himself. And this creature, Leviathan, has just one master. Only one can put a hook in its nose. Only one can make Leviathan into a pet for little girls. Only one can fill its hide with harpoons because everything under heaven belongs to him. Job's Lord is also Leviathan's Lord. This is the main gospel point: The Lord is the Lord of everything and everyone, even Leviathan. Getting to this gospel truth in the wake of trauma truly matters. It is one of several important truths that can move us to truly live again.

Vitezslav Gardavsky, a Czech philosopher, wrote that the terrible threat against life is not death or pain or trauma or disaster but rather "that we might die earlier than we really do die, before death becomes a natural necessity."[49] You see, Satan knows that after trauma, you are spiritually wounded as well as spiritually vulnerable. He has many tactics to keep you in your trauma, to make sure you do "die before you die." If he can keep you fearful, you will not step out or try or take risks again. He will use shame and guilt and doubt and confusion—whatever he can to keep you dead before you die.

One of Satan's favorite lies is "God is weak. He sympathizes with you. He cries with you, but he is helpless to put things right. He is powerless to get you the justice you so desperately crave." In the wake of violation, you crave justice and Satan promises you that you will never get it. The corporation that harmed you has too much money for you to make a dent in its bottom line with a lawsuit. That person who violated you will just lie about it, and it will be a "he said, she said" kind of case. The best Jesus can do for you is cry with you, Satan preaches.

A pastor told about a child abuse survivor who had gone to a counseling organization for help with post-traumatic living. The counselor advised the survivor, "I want you to imagine that as the abuse was going on, Jesus was in the corner, crying." When the survivor tried to picture it, he just felt worse. He did not need Jesus' tears at that moment. He needed the Lord of Leviathan to show up and set things right.

You see, sometimes we do not need or even want Jesus' tears. Sometimes what we need is for the Lord of Leviathan to show up. We crave for him to come in and stick a fishhook in its nose and lead it around. We want him to put a shock collar on Leviathan's neck, and obedience-train it too, so that even our three-year-old daughter can control it. We want the Lord of Leviathan to confront the fierce beast with an even fiercer weapon that can penetrate its body armor, making him more than just a harpoon cushion. Sometimes we need the Lord's powerful right arm. And that is exactly what Job chapter 41 gifts to us. It gifts to us the Lord of Leviathan.

Do not underestimate the Lord of Leviathan's power.

Leviathan did. It raged against Jesus, sending wave after demonic wave of fury and hate against the Holy One. When Jesus commanded "Be gone," the dark spirits had to flee. Satan himself entered the battle and tempted the Sinless One, but Jesus' determination to obey his Father sent the prince of darkness packing. Satan returned, entered Judas, and helped put Jesus on the cross. But once again, Satan had underestimated the Son. I can imagine the party in hell: Jesus died and Satan crowed to his minions, "I have done it! I have killed the Lord of life and now the world is all mine!" But he had underestimated Jesus because on the third day, the Lord of Leviathan rose again. The very first thing that Jesus did was descend into hell. He went straight into the enemy's lair to announce his victory: "Satan, I hold the field forever. Hell is your eternal home." Right then and there, justice was returning to the earth.

Sometimes we get a taste of this vindication. In the Netflix series *Unbelievable*,[50] the victims of a serial rapist have gathered for their attacker's sentencing. Will justice be done? The victims' impact statements have been delivered. All of them hold their breath as the judge announces that the rapist has been sentenced to 327.5 years. Immediately, the tension in the room dissolves, replaced by smiles and hugs all around. God has given the gift of justice, and Satan's lies have fallen flat. God had seen it. One final day awaits Mr. O'Leary when he will finally answer for his crimes. Jesus is the Lord who not only justifies us for our sins but also has promised to judge the living and the dead. He is the Lord of Leviathan. Leviathan is judged; the deed is done.

Here's another thing about Luther's hymn "A Mighty Fortress Is Our God." A question comes up about the end of the third stanza: "One little word can fell him." What is the "one little word" that can put a hook through Leviathan's nose and turn Satan into an obedient dog? Some people think it is the word *liar*.[51] When Satan taunts you, "Jesus certainly does love you. He is over there, crying in the corner," you can pull out the one little word and fire back, "Liar! Jesus certainly does love me and will rise up in my defense." And with that word, Satan must flee with his tail between his legs. Maybe the one little word is *liar*.

I prefer a different word, a little word that comes with the promise of righting all wrongs. This little word comes with the power to drive demons into pigs and send Satan to the fiery lake of burning sulfur where he belongs. One little word has that much power. I am going to write it now, and the forces of hell will tremble.

Jesus.

Postscript

If your trauma was public in any way or was suffered in service to your country, lawyers may invite themselves into your life. They may send you a packet that glimmers with the gold they promise you in the cover letter.

I cannot tell you whether you should engage an attorney or not. The details of your loss make that a determination only you can make in consultation with a qualified attorney and with prayer.

If you do pursue legal redress, make sure you do it for the right reasons. Don't do it out of greed or looking for vengeance. Both of these reasons can surface in any sinful heart. A right reason to engage an attorney would be to obtain compensation for real loss. For example, if you suffered physical or psychological harm that prevents you from working, you might rightfully seek compensation. You might also wish to prevent what you suffered from happening to anyone else.

Be aware that engaging an attorney might cost you emotionally and spiritually in ways you may be unable to quantify. It will be difficult for you to move through the stages of healing while settlement talks or litigation are pending. In conversations with your attorney and in the investigations that follow, you will constantly be reminded of your trauma. You may even be incentivized to report the gravest sort of injuries. In addition, your attorney may ask you to relive your experience repeatedly without thinking about the harm it causes you. Finally, if and when you walk away with a settlement or a jury award, you may very well feel a sense of emptiness. In fact, most survivors report an inexplicable sadness at receiving any kind of settlement money.

I tell you this so that you enter any attorney relationship with prayer and a good support system. You will be navigating spiritually difficult waters. Remember that even if you elect to pursue a claim in the courts, ultimately the Lord will get you justice for what you have suffered. Your groans rise up to heaven itself!

Ninth Letter

Overcome Evil With Good

Do not repay anyone evil for evil. Be careful to do what is right in the eyes of everyone. If it is possible, as far as it depends on you, live at peace with everyone. Do not take revenge, my dear friends, but leave room for God's wrath, for it is written: "It is mine to avenge; I will repay," says the Lord. On the contrary: "If your enemy is hungry, feed him; if he is thirsty, give him something to drink. In doing this, you will heap burning coals on his head."

Do not be overcome by evil, but overcome evil with good.

(Romans 12:17-21)

Dear Survivor,

Saul had thrown that spear at David on so many occasions, thrown it to kill him. As David stared at that spear—the one I like to think of as having "Saul" engraved on the handle—he remembered. He remembered the frequent summons into Saul's chamber to calm the king with a harp. Whenever the evil spirit from the Lord would come over Saul and torment him, David was tasked with playing his harp. "Then relief would come to Saul; he would feel better, and the evil spirit would leave him" (1 Samuel 16:23). But sometimes Saul worked himself into such anger that he would pick up the spear and try to inflict a mortal wound by pinning David to the wall with it. David, however, was a survivor. As he played, he would keep one eye on the harp and the other eye on the frown of the king. As Saul lunged for the spear, David would take evasive action and the spear would strike harmlessly into the wall. Then David would sing in his heart another prayer of thanksgiving to God for his salvation from such a hateful man.

Now David held that same spear—the king's personal weapon—in his hand. David had finally fled from Saul's court and was on the run. Saul then went out to hunt David down. In the night, however, David stole into the king's camp with Abishai. All of Saul's troops were fast asleep, and so was Saul, right in the middle of the camp. David and Abishai stood there next to the sleeping king and quietly considered what to do. There was Saul's own spear, stuck in the ground next to his head. Abishai pleaded for permission to use the spear to murder the monarch. Abishai was making a convincing argument. "Today God has delivered your enemy into your hands. Now let me pin him to the ground with one thrust of the spear; I won't strike him twice" (1 Samuel 26:8). But the permission was not granted, even though it would have allowed David to assume the throne. Instead of pursuing what seemed a sure thing, David lived in godly fear and faith, and he would not repay evil with evil. The man anointed by God to be the future king would not prematurely end the reign of the man anointed by God to be the current king. Saul's end was in the Lord's hands and the Lord's timing. Instead, David would try to overcome evil with good. After sneaking out of the camp with Saul's spear and water jug, David held the dreaded spear—and sent it back to Saul.

Can good really overcome evil? Or will evil always answer good with more evil?

In Romans 12:17-21, Paul teaches us to return good to those who cause us evil. Some have made the accusation that Paul didn't understand human nature—not really. How could he when he counsels us to answer evil with good? How could he when he urges survivors to forgive, even to do good to those who harmed them?

The apostle gives us no room to believe that it is okay to avoid our enemies, give them the silent treatment, or pretend they do not exist—not if these are forms of retaliation. Instead, he empowers us. Leave revenge up to God; overcome evil with good. Jesus' words echo: "I tell you, do not resist an evil person. If anyone slaps you on the right cheek, turn to them the other cheek also. And if anyone wants to sue you and take your shirt, hand over your coat as well" (Matthew 5:39,40). The message is the same: Overcome evil with good.

This is so counterintuitive. Our first reaction is to answer a slap with a slap, a lawsuit with a lawsuit, a spear with a spear, an insult with an insult, a power play with a power play. True evil will not be overcome by a kind gesture, we reason, so we must answer evil with evil. We must get revenge. We believe it is the only way to stay safe, the only way to defend ourselves, the only way to survive in a dog-eat-dog city. It lets people know that we mean business. It reminds people that they ought not mess with us again. Worldly wisdom tells you that it would be foolish to turn the other cheek.

But is it really wise to answer evil with evil? Is it safe? In Herman Melville's *Moby Dick,* Captain Ahab will stop at nothing to kill a great white sperm whale (Moby Dick) because it had bitten off his leg. In his revenge-crazed bloodlust, he risks everything. Captain Ahab finally harpoons Moby Dick, but the line gets tangled around the captain's neck. The great whale dives deep, and the two die together. Herman Melville understood the truth: In seeking revenge, you only destroy yourself.

How much emotional energy have you wasted by remembering your trauma and nursing your anger? How many productive, kind things go undone because you are trying to harpoon your own Moby Dick?

In answering evil with evil, we not only destroy ourselves, but we also make God our enemy. Do you really believe God loves it when we hold grudges? seek revenge? waste precious emotional energy and time on the past? How can we remain God's friend when God is love but we are attempting to fulfill our hate? It is not so wise to answer evil with evil, is it?

It is so human, so natural, to answer a spear thrown at you by throwing it back. At the same time, it is so divine, so supernatural, to answer evil with good. When I really think about it, it blows me away: Evil men take the hands of God's own Son and hold them to the wood. He does not struggle; he lets them pound nails into his hands and feet. They raise his cross into the air, satisfied they have taken his life. Actually, they have not taken his life. They cannot take what he willingly gives. He answers the hammer blows with a gentle prayer: "Father, forgive them, for they do not know what they are doing" (Luke 23:34). This is what God is like. He does not repay his enemies or seek vengeance. He prays for them. He dies for them. He saves them. When we were still his enemies, he died for us—for you. Even when we answer tit for tat, even when we become God's enemies, God's answer is always more patience, more grace, more gospel. "Father, forgive them." It is the same prayer he offers on our behalf every day. "Father, forgive them." He will. He does!

Does it seem foolish to pay back evil with good? Was Jesus a fool for answering evil with the ultimate good: giving his life? Not at all! It seemed like it when they laid his limp body in the tomb and his enemies rejoiced. But he rose from the dead, and good overcame evil. Was Jesus a fool for answering your evil with his good? Not at all! He changed you, turning you from his enemy into his friend. He overcame your evil with his good. Was David a fool for not turning the spear against Saul? Not at all! It seemed like it when Saul was the hunter and David was the prey, but in God's timing, Saul died in battle and David became king. Good overcame evil. Are you a fool for answering evil with good? Not at all! It might seem like it, but just wait and trust. Good will overcome evil. God will overcome evil and hold evildoers accountable. He has promised it.

Luther famously said, "We are Christs—with and without the apostrophe."[52] We are Christ's because through his merit and death, he bought us. We belong to him. He changed us from being enemies of God to being his dear children. We are Christs as well. Each of us, because we belong to Christ, now becomes a Christ to the world. We are Christ to our spouse. We are Christ to our children and grandchildren. We are Christ to our enemies and our abusers. We overcome evil with good and with prayer. We answer hatred by helping our enemies. We give them something to eat and drink. In doing so, we show them the love of Christ. Let us be Christs—with and without the apostrophe.

Postscript

I know Paul is asking a lot when he calls on you to overcome evil with good, when he calls on you to forgive as Christ has forgiven you. I cannot understand what you have suffered. Paul could not either, although he suffered brutal attacks and grievous wounds during his own life.

You might be hoping I will tell you exactly how to forgive someone who did something unspeakable to you or how to remember the person differently or how to show kindness, if that is even safe to do. I understand that. I wish I had those answers for you, but I do not. God may have placed other people in your life who can offer you that kind of wisdom, including professional Christian counselors.

And yet I do trust the power of the gospel. I have seen and heard Christians forgive the very worst. One example was a segment of *60 Minutes* that featured interviews with survivors of mass shootings. Each had suffered grievous loss. A family member or fellow worshiper had been gunned down in cold blood. Each was asked, "Do you forgive the person for doing it?" Those who were Christian all answered tearfully that they had forgiven the murderer. But when someone of another faith was asked, the answer was no. What a testimony to the power of the gospel in the lives of Christians. It is possible to do some kind of good to someone who has caused trauma, though it may not be clear what that should be. Your loving Savior will help you understand as you seek the answers.

Part Three
Reconnection

Tenth Letter

Sheep, Dogs, or More Than Conquerors?

Who shall separate us from the love of Christ? Shall trouble or hardship or persecution or famine or nakedness or danger or sword? As it is written:

"For your sake we face death all day long; we are considered as sheep to be slaughtered."

No, in all these things we are more than conquerors through him who loved us. For I am convinced that neither death nor life, neither angels nor demons, neither the present nor the future, nor any powers, neither height nor depth, nor anything else in all creation, will be able to separate us from the love of God that is in Christ Jesus our Lord.

(Romans 8:35-39)

Dear Survivor,

The apostle Paul is asking a genuine question. I think sometimes we can miss that as we read this part of Romans chapter 8, because in this section he asks several questions that are not really questions. They are more like declarations. Grammar geeks call these rhetorical questions. These are questions that do not really expect an answer but are asked for effect. "If God is for us, who can be against us?" (Romans 8:31). Of course, the answer is nobody! "He who did not spare his own Son, but gave him up for us all—how will he not also, along with him, graciously give us all things?" (Romans 8:32). The answer, of course, is: He certainly will give us all things! These are not really questions but confident declarations.

In verse 35, however, we have a very real question: "Who shall separate us from the love of Christ?" Paul is really asking us the question.[53]

What about trouble? Do external circumstances that press down on your life like a trash compactor separate you from Jesus' love? What about persecution? Does someone who mocks you for your Christian faith separate you from Jesus' love? What about nakedness? Does spending a winter without adequate housing and sufficient clothing for the bitter cold separate you from Jesus' love? What about danger? Does assault or a near-death experience separate you from Jesus' love? What about the sword? Is a gunshot wound to the chest the last straw that proclaims Jesus truly does not love you? Paul presses the question so hard into our hearts that he names—count them—17 potential separators, 17 different violent assaults on your dignity and life. Does any of these things, he asks, separate you from God's love?

The world has a considered judgment on this question. They consider that such a person who has suffered any one of these potential separators has been cut off from God's love. "But is that true?" the apostle asks.

I cannot erase the disturbing image of a slaughterhouse. A long line of sheep awaits a quick and brutal end. These sheep are considered worthless. Some are weak, frail, or sick. Others are just not productive anymore. The world has marked these sheep for slaughter. They seem beyond healing and love, vulnerable, and easy marks for abuse, devouring, or the trash heap. The world, in its considered judgment, sees worthless sheep. Is that what God sees too: sheep broken and ready for the trash heap? Is that the way we see ourselves: sheep that everyone else just abuses?

A very sad and provocative experiment was designed to observe how trauma impacted dogs. Some dogs were locked in cages that were repeatedly electrified while the doors to the cages remained closed and locked. At first, the dogs tried to get out of the cages, but eventually the traumatized dogs just lay down and endured the painful shocks. In the next phase of the study, the researchers opened the cage doors of the traumatized dogs as well as the doors of a second group of dogs that had not been previously shocked. Then they shocked all of the dogs. The ones that had never been shocked before walked right out of the electrified cages. Do you know what the traumatized dogs did? They just lay in their electrified cages with the doors wide open. They had come to consider themselves as nothing more than victims, as sheep marked for slaughter. This was now their life. Is this really who we are?[54]

No! Paul will not have it. He knows that is not who we are. He urges us to throw off the opinions of those who view us as victims, as sheep marked for slaughter or as traumatized dogs, because that is not who we are.

Do you realize that Romans 8:35-39 is one big, verbal, Christ-filled hug? This section opens by asking if anything can separate us from the One who died for us; it closes by answering that nothing in all creation can separate us from the love of God in Christ. And in the middle, it proclaims that we are more than conquerors through the One who loved us. This is the big, verbal, Christ-filled hug that you get here in Romans chapter 8.[55]

But it is more than a mere verbal or literary hug. This warm embrace by God himself in Christ is as real as it gets. Survivor, you appreciate, perhaps better than everyone else, how one event can shape and form you. You truly understand how there is a before and after. Sometimes the before and after of an event have emotional, spiritual, and physical impacts.

I know people who have experienced an event that caused them to face life in a wheelchair or lose their hearing or undergo repeated surgeries. We get that. But Paul wants you to know there is an event that impacted your life on an even larger scale. In fact, all of human history is divided into before Christ and after Christ. Every Christian's life is similarly divided. The events of Christ's birth, death, and resurrection have eternal impact. When you come to know that the love of Christ is for you, life will never be the same. Those events of Christ have marked you as infinitely loved by God.

Can you see what I am saying? You are not defined by your trauma. Victimhood cannot define you. Influence you? Yes. Your traumatic experience will certainly leave lasting marks on your life and maybe on your body, but it is not the center of your identity. The most important thing about you is not that you were assaulted or were in a terrible accident or are disabled. It is not that your name is tarnished because of a trauma you caused to another or that you were targeted in a mass shooting or that you were interviewed on CNN. What is most important is that you are a beloved child of God. If anything in the past is going to define you, let it be this: God has loved you and forgiven you in Christ, and he has stored up for you an inheritance in heaven where all things will be made new. You are deeply loved in Christ, and that is the most important thing about you!

I want to return with you to the story about those poor, traumatized dogs. The researchers next wondered how they could help the dogs reclaim their lives. How could the dogs learn they were no longer victims but could actually leave the electrified cages? The answer was to gently and firmly help the dogs up and lead them out. They had to show the dogs physically that they were no longer victims but were loved and had their own agency. And when the dogs were loved like that, they reclaimed their lives. When their unlocked cages were electrified again, the dogs left on their own. They threw off their victimhood and reclaimed their lives and their identities as fighters. They were no longer sheep to be slaughtered. They were conquerors.

And now we have arrived at Paul's big finish. We know who we are through the One who loved us. The apostle Paul is so triumphant on this point. We are even more than conquerors or champions or victors. We exceed the greatest heroes and victors that history can name because all that Christ won for us is now ours. Forgiveness is ours. Life is ours. Purpose is ours. The kingdom of heaven is ours. Everything is ours through Christ who loved us! Everyone and everything else are trivial in comparison. Nothing else marks our lives quite like that. And since this new status is ours and these things can never be taken from us, we can join the apostle's defiant declaration that we are hard-pressed but not crushed, confused but not abandoned, traumatized but not destroyed (2 Corinthians 4:7-12). When we get knocked down, the life of Jesus in us gives us strength to get back up again. We were once victims but not anymore. We are not merely survivors, although we are that too. We are conquerors and more. That is our new identity in Christ.

Eleventh Letter

Survivor's Mission

When they had finished eating, Jesus said to Simon Peter, "Simon son of John, do you love me more than these?"

"Yes, Lord," he said, "you know that I love you."

Jesus said, "Feed my lambs."

(John 21:15)

Dear Survivor,

Knowing your mission is important. Members of the military know that before they launch an operation, they need to understand the mission. This is also why the military fears so much what they call mission creep: the gradual, even unconscious, shift in mission goals. The church also understands this. It is why churches spend time developing mission statements. A church without a mission could be described as a church without a heartbeat, but a church with a mission has a spring in its step. Mission is essential to your life too as a survivor living a post-traumatic life.

Viktor Frankl spoke powerfully about post-traumatic mission. In his book *Man's Search for Meaning*[56] Dr. Frankl describes how he and others survived Auschwitz and other concentration camps during World War II. Although he narrates real horrors, he also tells the story with scientific objectivity. He noticed that some prisoners died quickly, even though they were physically stronger and more robust than he was. Others survived despite the fact that they were physically wasting away. He could only account for the difference by looking at the spiritual. He concluded that in order to survive the hell of the camps, you needed a why. We might call it a purpose or a mission. He wrote, "Those who have a *why* to live can bear with almost any *how*."

Purpose, mission, a why—this is essential to life, especially for those who have endured trauma. That is what Jesus gives us with these words. He gives us a survivor's mission, one that is personal, springs from love, and is just the right size. Let's look separately at each of these aspects of the survivor's mission.

First, Jesus offers Simon Peter a survivor's mission that is personal. After hauling in a miraculous catch of fish and sharing a breakfast prepared by the risen Savior, things turn serious for Peter. Jesus addresses him by his full name—Simon son of John—and Peter immediately knows that whatever Jesus says next has important meaning for his life. When someone picks you out of a crowd and calls you by name, you sense he or she has something important, perhaps very personal, to share. That sense increases when this person uses your full name, as Jesus does here. He does not call him Peter, or Cephas, but uses his "birth certificate" name. When someone calls me Timothy Carl Bourman, I know I had better perk up because a personal word is coming my way. Jesus is about to give Simon a mission. This mission was not for all the Simons of the world, nor for all the apostles, but just for Simon son of John.

Later, Simon was curious about the mission assigned to his fellow apostle John, so he asked, "Lord, what about him?" (John 21:21). Jesus brought Simon right back to his own personal mission with a penetrating question: "What is that to you? You must follow me" (John 21:22). In other words, "You need to stay focused on what I have given you to do. John has his own personal mission."

This is our first point: Your God-given mission is something only you can carry out. It cannot be any other Simon in the world who carries out your mission. Your purpose has only your name on it. Once you have this point clear, the Spirit can begin to show you your unique mission. As an example, only I can be a Christian husband for my wife, Amanda. Only I can be a Christian father to my children. Only I am the called pastor at my church, and so on. God has given me a special set of gifts and experiences. All of this comes together to put my name on a personal mission that only Timothy Carl Bourman can carry out in this world. And the same is true for you. Jesus has placed you into unique relationships with others and given you unique experiences. All of this makes your mission from Jesus personal.

So far, we have agreed that your mission is something only you can carry out, but none of this yet makes your mission godly or good in any way. Jesus knew Simon son of John would need more guidance in his mission than the name on his birth certificate. So Jesus asks, "Simon son of John, do you love me?" Now I want you to notice something about this question. Jesus could have just said, "Simon, here is your mission." But he needs to ask this question for Peter's own sake: "Simon son of John, do you love me?" Please understand something. There was no doubt that Jesus loved the brash fisherman. He had gone all the way to the cross for Peter and then rose and appeared to this disciple to personally forgive him for his cowardly denial of his master, recorded in Mark 14:66-72. It was now time for Peter to look at his own motivations. "Simon son of John, do you love me?" Three times Jesus asks him, perhaps echoing the three times Peter had disowned him.

You see, Peter could have easily approached his mission with the wrong heart. He could have gone out of guilt or shame. He might have been motivated to make up for what he had done wrong or to convince the other disciples to believe he was a changed man. But Jesus wants Peter to serve for only one reason. "Simon son of John, do you love me?"

Do you love Jesus? There can be no doubt that he loves you. He lived for you. He died for you. He put his name on you in Baptism and places his own body and blood on your lips with his Holy Supper. Do you love him? Does everything you do spring from this love? Jesus wants your mission to spring from love for him who loved you first.

What was Peter's mission? "Feed my lambs." He was to care for the little ones whom Jesus had bought with his own blood. He was to share with them the Word of Life. He was to bring them spiritual meal after spiritual meal until he could not anymore. It would seem easy to feed the lambs a couple times a day. You might expect Jesus to give a man like Peter a bigger, more impressive mission. Yet this is not a small mission. He was to care gently and carefully for the young ones, just as Jesus had cared for him. This mission was not too big or too small. It was just the right size.

This was a Goldilocks kind of mission. Do you remember that story? Goldilocks didn't like the really big thing or the really small thing. She needed something that was just right. This is especially important for survivors of trauma. Typically, survivors struggle to reengage in life and relationships in a healthy way. Some survivors are reluctant to reengage at all. Maybe they feel guilt or shame or inadequacy because of what they have suffered. As a result, their idea of mission is too small. Other survivors may feel that since they have been given a new lease on life, they had better make full use of the little time they have left. I have heard about survivors uprooting their entire lives to move across the country or even to foreign countries, all in an effort to give back. Such a mission may prove too big.

What about a mission that is just right for you? What about a mission that flows from your love for Jesus, who loved you first? What about a mission that's designed specifically for you with your skills, interests, and experiences? And all of this so you and your Savior can bring about lasting, eternal, and spiritual results? That might look as simple as serving in your church, teaching Sunday school, or leading your family in devotions. It may not be a glamorous mission. It may not make you famous or rich, but it matters, just like "Feed my lambs."

Start with what is at the very core of importance and work your way out. What do you need to do before you die? What is at the heart of it all? When everything else melts away and nothing is left, there is only one thing that matters: that we are loved by Jesus and that those closest to us know his saving name too. Thinking about the ultimate goal in life brings that kind of clarity and results in a mission that is personal, springs from love, and is just the right size.

Twelfth Letter

Inscribed

On that day HOLY TO THE LORD will be inscribed on the bells of the horses, and the cooking pots in the LORD's house will be like the sacred bowls in front of the altar. Every pot in Jerusalem and Judah will be holy to the LORD Almighty, and all who come to sacrifice will take some of the pots and cook in them. And on that day there will no longer be a Canaanite in the house of the LORD Almighty.

(Zechariah 14:20,21)

Dear Survivor,

This is it—the grand finale to Zechariah's great book. If this were the July 4th fireworks display, this would be the part where there is an explosion of color in the sky. These two verses close out a powerful and dramatic book. There you find supersonic horses (6:1-8), a kind of exorcism of Satan who stood beside Joshua (3:1-10), and a military operation that included airlifting out of Israel a woman named Wickedness (5:5-11). You even find King Jesus riding into his own city on a donkey (9:9,10) and a fountain to cleanse the people of sin (13:1). Zechariah wrote a book of vivid prophetic imagery, concluding with these amazing words in 14:20,21.

Are you disappointed with the ending? Were you hoping for more? Zechariah has his critics. Some Bible scholars, like unkind critics after the closing scene of a great show, label these final verses #finalefail. They want more from Zechariah. Some critics get nasty about the bells. One commentator mocked them, calling them "superfluous little bells."[57] Is the criticism justified? Zechariah has not mentioned bells before this. Why now? Are they truly superfluous? Nonessential? Why is Zechariah talking about them?

Others are even more disappointed with Zechariah's reference to cookware. The only other times the Scriptures discuss kitchen cookery with any depth are in Exodus and Leviticus when Moses discusses the items used for worship at the temple. Some wonder why Zechariah would get stuck on items that might appear on a wedding registry. Why are we talking about mundane pots and bowls at the end of Zechariah's spectacular, jarring, dramatic book? And why am I getting stuck on it in this letter to you?

Because this is how I am closing my book too.

As I thought about this finale to the book of Zechariah, I imagined these "superfluous, mundane" items debating their own importance and whether they were essential. The conversation went a little like the conversation the apostle Paul imagined in 1 Corinthians 12:14-21 taking place between different body parts. Maybe you know the conversation I am talking about, in which the eye, staking its claim to its own importance as essential in the body, says to the hand, "I don't need you!" Meanwhile, the foot, so depressed about its importance, says to itself, "I'm not needed. I quit being a part of the body." My imaginary conversation was between household items.

I imagined the garbage can boasting to the tinkling bells, "I collect garbage and make sure the house doesn't fill up with stink." And the bells, depressed to be so unimportant, grumble to the garbage can, "You're right—we stink. Open your mouth. We'll jump in." Then the bowls turn on the pots, "We don't really need you around. You just take up space." Poor bells. Poor pots. It is devasting to be called superfluous, unwanted, nonessential.

During the COVID-19 pandemic, this talk came to the forefront like I have never seen in my lifetime. Many vocations were labeled either essential or nonessential. I understand that government leaders faced difficult decisions, but the vocabulary they used was heartless and caused real spiritual damage. Doctors, nurses, and liquor vendors were termed essential, but artists, teachers, and pastors were not. By labeling such vocations nonessential, the people filling them sensed a downgrading of their value and importance, even as human beings. Other people suddenly felt valued and wanted. One woman posted on Facebook, "I work as a phlebotomist. It's about time that people remember that we exist." *The Sunday Times* published a survey asking which jobs were most essential and which were nonessential.[58] Health care, of course, came in as the number one essential job. Artist came in at the bottom as the least essential job. Artists flipped out and pushed back. "Fine," they said, "then turn off Netflix and Spotify and get rid of your TVs." So we dehumanized people and told them their work was superfluous, unwanted, and nonessential.

I wonder, though, if we have always felt that way about our various vocations. We have just never said it out loud. The stay-at-home parent has fought this notion for decades. What did Dad do all day while his lawyer wife was off defending her clients? He managed to change a few diapers, shop for groceries, and keep the kids alive for one more day. The budget analyst who inputs numbers into a system most of the day wonders what good she does, if any at all. The line worker does not feel much better as he slaughters chickens in the poultry factory.

The truth is that sensitive believers want to serve God and their neighbor. Sensitive believers want to impact the world. Sensitive believers want their work to matter well beyond a paycheck, but many feel like they do not. Studs Terkel wrote a landmark book, *Working*, about work life in the United States. In the introduction, he explained, "It is, above all, about daily humiliations. To survive the day is triumph enough for the walking wounded among the great many of us."[59] It turns out that the vast majority of us had already deemed our vocations as nonessential. The pandemic made many wonder, "Do I need a career change? Is my job valuable to God and others? Or is it nothing more than a tinkling bell or mundane and ordinary like pots and pans?"

You might be wondering why am I writing about bells and pots and bowls at the end of a book on trauma. I will tell you. After trauma, the decibel level on these questions about purpose and usefulness goes up, way up. The questions are screamed. You may think that because you lived, because you survived, God must have some great purpose for you and that certainly cannot involve returning to the same drab life as before. I have heard about survivors who cannot—will not—return to their very ordinary lives. The veteran returns from war but cannot stand "just" driving trucks. He quits his job and his family to walk across the United States or to do good in South America. It is hard to move from extraordinary to ordinary. It is hard to move back into the daily grind of day in and day out service to others. It feels nonessential, superfluous, and you are convinced that God wants something great out of you. Your trauma demands it.

Survivor, it will be hard. You are coming off an extraordinary event. Returning to life means returning to the normal and the ordinary.

That is why I want to discuss bells and bowls and pots and pans with you. Zechariah foresaw a day when all distinctions would be erased. On that day, there would be no distinction between the superfluous and the indispensable. On that day, there would be no distinction between the sacred and the secular. On that day, there would be no distinction between nonessential and essential because on that day everyone and everything would be inscribed with "Holy to the LORD," even the little bells and the bowls and pots. Anyone who tried to undermine God's holiness, like the unbelieving Canaanites often did, would have no place, would not be welcome in God's family. Zechariah could see the day in the distance—a day when everyone and everything would be "holy to the LORD."

Zechariah saw it from a distance, glimpses of how it would happen. In one vision, he saw Israel's humble King ride into Jerusalem on a donkey (Zechariah 9:9,10). In another vision, he saw Israel mourning because they had pierced their God (Zechariah 12:10-14), followed by another vision of a fountain that bubbled up in the middle of Jerusalem and cleansed the inhabitants from sin and impurity (Zechariah 13:1). Finally, he saw the Shepherd of Israel struck down and the sheep scattered, but resulting in God identifying those of whom he would say, "They are my people," who would in turn say, "The LORD is our God" (Zechariah 13:7-9). Zechariah saw all of these glimpses of the coming Messiah Jesus.

We too have seen him ride into Jerusalem, determined to pay the awful price for the sin of the world. We have seen him pierced with nails and later with a spear. We have seen his blood-spouting hands and feet become a cleansing fountain, making sinners "holy to the LORD." The day Zechariah saw in the distance has arrived. Jesus has arrived. Today is that day.

Luther understood this—and then saw something else when it comes to our work as God's forgiven people: Jesus has bled all over us and what we do to make it holy.[60] Luther's doctrine of vocation, or calling, which he drew from the Scriptures, was revolutionary in his day. For him, there was no distinction between the sacred and the secular or between the essential and nonessential because Jesus has bled over all of it. He famously quipped, "God milks the cows through the callings of the milk maids."[61] Someone has to milk the cows. Someone has to change diapers. Someone has to create art. When it comes to his people and their godly efforts for him, all of it is holy to the Lord. God is in all of it. Frederick Buechner wrote, "Where our deep gladness meets the world's need, there is our calling." When our deep gladness springs from the rescue mission of our Savior and what that means to us, the work we do in our various vocations is hardly mundane and unimportant.[62] Jesus has bled over all of it, and all of it is holy to the Lord.

I challenge you to reimagine your life. You may have to work at it to see what you do as God sees it, but it will be worth the effort. I challenge you to inscribe everything you do with the initials HTTL. If people ask you what it means, tell them it means "Holy to the LORD." If you clean toilets, label them as HTTL when you finish. If you write code or do homework or burp babies or deliver mail or butcher cows or teach children or build buildings, inscribe all of it with HTTL, "Holy to the LORD." When you do that, a couple of things will happen. You will end up doing everything to the very best of your ability because you will realize that you are the hands and feet of God and what you are doing is sacred. A second thing will happen. You will also see that what you do matters. Not only is it holy to the Lord because Jesus has bled on it, but it is also important to your neighbor. It is a service, an act of love, and that makes you an essential worker.

There is genius in the way that Zechariah closes his book. His book is full of the dramatic and the extraordinary, including glimpses of the messianic future and all that the sacrifice of Jesus means. But then he ends his book in this way, and in doing so, depicts the ordinary as extraordinary for God's people. He makes the nonessential essential. He makes the secular sacred. He makes every moment of our lives matter, even the parts that tinkle like bells.

epilogue

Dear Survivor,

I want to give you some insight into how these letters are woven together. The basic flow of the letters follows the three-step model in Judith Herman's *Trauma and Recovery*. In a new release of her text in 2015, Herman canonizes this approach. "The model of recovery stages proposed in this book has held up remarkably well over two decades and is now widely recognized as the foundation of trauma treatment."[63] Herman's three stages of recovery are (1) safety, (2) remembrance and mourning, and (3) reconnection.[64] My letters come alongside you, Survivor, as you move through these stages of recovery.[65]

Safety

Healing begins by establishing safety in all its facets. For example, safety means you must first be removed from an abusive situation. However, safety extends much further. It includes (1) finding safety in your body, (2) moving toward finding a safe environment, and (3) engaging in safe relationships.

Safety in your own body is established first through basic medical care. Once this care has been provided, the work begins to give you back control of your body. This includes dealing with intrusion and hyperarousal. Sometimes medications can be prescribed that "block the action of the sympathetic nervous system."[66] Therapies useful for this stage of recovery include body-based techniques like yoga.[67] Also, techniques to ground yourself in the present, such as mindfulness or meditation, have proliferated. These help you use your senses to ground yourself, especially when experiencing a flashback.

Remembrance and Mourning

Once you have established safety in your body, spaces, and relationships, you can begin stage two of recovery. At this point, you are tasked with telling your trauma story. The point of telling the story is not to retraumatize you but rather to transform the event and give it meaning. This telling of the trauma story will allow you to integrate the memory back into the normal flow of life.[68] This work of reconstructing the story and transforming it is essential to recovery. It is also challenging because the traumatic memory is wordless, frozen, and fragmented.

> The traumatic event challenges you to become a theologian, a philosopher, and a jurist. You are called upon to articulate the values and beliefs that you hold and apply them to the traumatic event. Survivors of atrocity of every age and culture come to a point in their testimony where all questions are reduced to one, spoken more in bewilderment than outrage: Why? The answer is beyond human understanding. Beyond this unfathomable question, you must also confront another equally incomprehensible question: Why me? The arbitrary, random quality of your fate seems to defy a predictable world order.[69]

I hope these letters have brought God's Word to you in such a way that you are able to bear your own story and tell it. The opening letters in Part Two speak especially to this need for storytelling.

After you have told your trauma story in detail and with emotion, transforming the memory, you are ready for the second part of stage two: mourning. You are called to name all that has been lost and what can never be recovered. In this part of recovery, you admit you are grieving spiritual, physical, and emotional loss. At this point, you may also have to wrestle with the concept of justice and the role of the lawsuit. Interaction with lawyers will almost always complicate the mourning process. You may vacillate between deep sadness and anger.

Reconnection

Reconnection is the last stage in trauma recovery. This stage can only happen after safety has been established in the present and the memory of the past has been transformed. At this point, you are ready to address the future. You may need to unlearn any learned helplessness and work at regaining your personal agency. You will need to connect with others in your community. You will need a sense of mission and deep purpose in the world. Some survivors will find joy in discovering a survivor mission. Turning the trauma into good for the world can help give meaning to the trauma. While "resolution is never complete . . . the best indices of resolution are the survivor's restored capacity to take pleasure in her life and to engage fully in relationships with others."[70]

I began this book on a very personal note as I described what it was like for me to wake up with a traumatic memory in my head. I yearned for a pensieve like Harry Potter's to sift my memories, but no such thing was available. What I should have yearned for was not the wave of a magic wand but instead a stack of letters much like this book.

Survivor, this resource was important for me in carrying out part of God's deep purpose in my own experience of trauma. These letters were born out of deep pain, many tears, and a profound joy that found me even in my suffering. The old aphorism is true: God never wastes a hurt. Your turn.

Yours in Jesus,
TCB

endnotes

1   A basin used to store and review memories. J. K. Rowling, *Harry Potter and the Goblet of Fire* (New York: Scholastic Books, 2002).

2   "SAMHSA's Concept of Trauma and Guidance for a Trauma-Informed Approach," Substance Abuse and Mental Health Services Administration, https://store.samhsa.gov/sites/default/files/d7/priv/sma14-4884.pdf (accessed July 31, 2019), p. 7.

3   It is for this reason that the DSM-5 lists as "Criteria A" for the diagnosis of PTSD the following features of an event: "The person was exposed to: death, threatened death, actual or threatened serious injury, or actual or threatened sexual violence, as follows: 1. Direct exposure. 2. Witnessing, in person. 3. Indirectly, by learning that a close relative or close friend was exposed to trauma. If the event involved actual or threatened death, it must have been violent or accidental. 4. Repeated or extreme indirect exposure to aversive details of the event(s), usually in the course of professional duties (e.g., first responders collecting body parts; professionals repeatedly exposed to details of child abuse). This does not include indirect non-professional exposure through electronic media, television, movies or pictures." *Diagnostic and Statistical Manual of Mental Disorders: DSM-5* (Arlington: American Psychiatric Association, 2013).

4   Although not recognized as widely, some Christians have provided additional insight into PTSD, PTS, or PTL. The condition is framed in this way by two Christian psychologists. "A whole-person response to traumatic events that encompasses the physical, mental, emotional, behavioral, and spiritual being of those affected. It results in significant disruption of life in the home, work, school, and church. It often draws on anger, fear, sadness, shame, and guilt to disrupt family relationships, friendships, careers, and Christian service. Those who are affected will often compensate the best they can in ways that compound the struggle they face." Curtis Solomon, "Ministering to PTSD: Demystifying PTSD," produced by the Institute for Biblical Counseling and Discipleship, podcast, MP3 audio, 10:43–11:12, https://ibcd.org/demystifying-ptsd/.Solomon.

5   Judith Lewis Herman, *Trauma and Recovery: The Aftermath of Violence, from Domestic Abuse to Political Terror* (New York: Basic Books, 1992), p. 37.

6   Herman, *Trauma and Recovery*, p. 42.

7   Bessel A. Van der Kolk, *The Body Keeps the Score: Brain, Mind, and Body in the Healing of Trauma* (New York: Penguin Books, 2015), pp. 51-53. Van der Kolk describes a little boy named Noam who was not traumatized during 9/11 because he retained his personal agency. He was able to run away from the falling towers.

8   Herman, *Trauma and Recovery*, p. 42.

9   Herman, *Trauma and Recovery*, p. 35.

10   Herman, *Trauma and Recovery*, p. 36.

11   N. Duncan Sinclair, *Horrific Traumata: A Pastoral Response to the Post-Traumatic Stress Disorder* (Philadelphia: Haworth Press, 1993), p. 66.

[12] Sinclair, *Horrific Traumata*, p. 66.

[13] Kathleen O'Connor, *Jeremiah: Pain and Promise* (Minneapolis: Fortress Press, 2012), pp. 25,26.

[14] Kristin A. Vargas, *How Long, O Lord: Hope and Help When You Have Been Deeply Hurt* (St. Louis: Concordia Publishing House, 2018), p. 10.

[15] Vargas defines moral injury as "the distress that results from human beings committing, seeing, or experiencing acts that go against their beliefs of what is morally right and wrong. Moral injury is a crisis of conscience." Vargas, *How Long*, p. 11.

[16] David M. Blankenship, "Five Efficacious Treatments for Posttraumatic Stress Disorder: An Empirical Review," *Journal of Mental Health Counseling*, Vol. 39, No. 4 (2017), pp. 275-288.

[17] Blankenship, "Five Treatments," p. 278.

[18] Blankenship, "Five Treatments," p. 280.

[19] Blankenship, "Five Treatments," p. 282.

[20] Blankenship, "Five Treatments," p. 282.

[21] Large Catechism I,101-2, *The Book of Concord: The Confessions of the Evangelical Lutheran Church*, edited by Robert Kolb and Timothy J. Wengert (Minneapolis: Augsburg Fortress Press, 2000), p. 400.

[22] Vargas, *How Long*. Scholars seem to disagree about whether PTSD is primarily a spiritual, physiological, or psychological disorder. Regardless of where the problem primarily lies, I believe that the spiritual losses caused by trauma can be successfully addressed by God's Word and the Spirit working through it. Vargas has a very helpful discussion on the relationship between PTSD and moral injury on pages 15-22. She has a nice visual on page 20.

[23] Kathleen O'Connor, *Lamentations and the Tears of the World* (Maryknoll, New York: Orbis Books, 2002), p. 14. O'Connor gives this name to the female voice in her commentary. She has provided the unique insight that this is the first time the narrator addresses the city-woman.

[24] "Facts About Women and Trauma," American Psychological Association, https://www.apa.org/advocacy/interpersonal-violence/women-trauma (accessed July 31, 2019).

[25] David Finkelhor, et al., "Sexual Abuse in a National Survey of Adult Men and Women: Prevalence, Characteristics, and Risk Factors," *Child Abuse and Neglect*, Vol. 14, No. 1 (1990), pp. 19-28.

[26] "How Common Is PTSD in Adults?" National Center for PTSD, US Department of Veterans Affairs, https://www.ptsd.va.gov/understand/common/common_adults.asp (accessed March 22, 2023).

[27] O'Connor, *Lamentations and the Tears*, p. 38.

[28] O'Connor, *Jeremiah: Pain and Promise*, pp. 2,3.

[29] Vargas, *How Long*, p. 52.

[30] M. Elizabeth Lewis Hall, "Suffering in God's Presence: The Role of Lament in Transformation," *Journal of Spiritual Formation and Soul Care*, Vol. 9, No. 2 (November 2016), p. 230.

[31] Herman, *Trauma and Recovery*, p. 171.

[32] Van der Kolk, *The Body Keeps the Score*, p. 84.

[33] Philip Yancey, *Where Is God When It Hurts?* (Grand Rapids: Zondervan, 1990), pp. 16-19.

[34] Martin Luther, *Luther's Works*, edited by Jaroslav Pelikan and Helmut T. Lehmann, American Edition, Vol. 31 (St. Louis: Concordia Publishing House; Philadelphia: Fortress Press, 1955–1986), p. 40.

35 *Luther's Works*, Vol. 33, p. 140.

36 *Luther's Works*, Vol. 1, p. 11.

37 John Schaller, "The Hidden God," Wisconsin Lutheran Seminary Essay File, http://wlsessays.net/handle/ 123456789/2027 (accessed July 11, 2020).

38 Samuel Degner, "Christian Apologetics in a Post/Modern Context," *Wisconsin Lutheran Quarterly*, Vol. 117, No. 2 (2020), p. 100.

39 Alvin Plantinga, *God, Freedom, and Evil* (Grand Rapids: Wm. B. Eerdmans Publishing Co., 1977), p. 30, quoted in Degner, "Christian Apologetics," p. 100.

40 Degner, "Christian Apologetics," p. 101.

41 Diane Langberg, *Suffering and the Heart of God: How Trauma Destroys and Christ Restores* (Greensboro, North Carolina: New Growth Press, 2015), p. 133.

42 Harold Senkbeil, *The Care of Souls* (Bellingham, Washington: Lexham, 2019), p. 138.

43 Langberg, *Suffering and the Heart of God*, p. 126.

44 Barbara Marcolini, "A Son Grapples with Guilt: Did He Give His Father the Coronavirus?" *New York Times*, https://www.nytimes.com/video/world/europe/ 100000007064635/italy-coronavirus-family-death.html (accessed July 11, 2020).

45 Adam Linehan, "I Watched Friends Die in Afghanistan. The Guilt Has Nearly Killed Me." *New York Times Magazine*, https://www.nytimes.com/2019/11/11/magazine/ survivor-guilt-veteran.html (accessed August 3, 2020).

46 Martin Luther, "A Mighty Fortress Is Our God," #201 in *Christian Worship: A Lutheran Hymnal* (Milwaukee: Northwestern Publishing House, 1993).

[47] I owe a deep debt of gratitude to my twin brother, Rev. Jonathan Bourman, for sharing with me his ideas on this text. He preached on this text first. That sermon, preached on February 10, 2019, can be found at this podcast/recording: "Coming Forth in Golden Victory: A Sermon Based on Job 41," produced by Peace Lutheran: http://www. peaceinaiken.com/sermons/tag/Job.

[48] Roy B. Zuck, *Sitting with Job: Selected Studies on the Book of Job* (Eugene, Oregon: Wipf and Stock, 2003), p. 375.

[49] Eugene H. Peterson, *Run with the Horses: The Quest for Life at Its Best* (InterVarsity, 2009), p. 21.

[50] *Unbelievable*, season 1, episode 8, directed by Susannah Grant, featuring Toni Collette, Merritt Wever, and Kaitlyn Dever, aired September 13, 2019 on Netflix.

[51] Two good blog posts address this historical question about Luther's one little word: Bryce Young, "What One Little Word Can Fell Satan?" *desiringGod*, August 20, 2017, https://www.desiringgod.org/articles/what-one-little-word-will-fell-satan. Jonathan Bauer, "What's the Word?" *WELS Hymnal Project*, November 1, 2015, http://welshymnal.com/blog/whats-word.

[52] *Luther's Works*, Vol 22, p. x.

[53] Michael Middendorf makes this point. "While the question in 8:32 began with 'will he not...?' which demands a positive answer, the intended answer to the question which opens 8:35 is not indicated." Michael P. Middendorf, *Romans 1-8*, Concordia Commentary (St. Louis: Concordia, 2016), p. 719.

[54] Van der Kolk, *The Body Keeps the Score*, p. 30.

[55] Middendorf comments on the important shift of vocabulary at the end of Romans chapter 8. "Thus the threefold use of love in 8:35, 37, 39, is emphatic and thematic." Middendorf, *Romans 1–8*, p. 718.

[56] Victor E. Frankl, *Man's Search for Meaning* (Boston: Beacon Press, 2006).

[57] Konrad R. Schaefer, "The Ending of the Book of Zechariah; A Commentary," *Revue Biblique*, Vol. 100, No. 2 (1946), p. 233.

[58] Stephen Tracy, "Milieu Insight Response and Clarification on The Sunday Times Essential Workers Poll," Milieu, https://mili.eu/insights/sunday-times-essential-workers-poll-response (accessed August 6, 2020).

[59] Studs Terkel, *Working* (New York: The New Press, 1974), p. xi.

[60] Mark Paustian's essay "Unleashing Our Calling: Today's Christians Find Fulfillment in Their Vocations" impacted this letter and my own thoughts on vocation incredibly. I am indebted to his essay not only in terms of vocabulary and thoughtful comments but also for pointing me to diverse resources and even these verses from Zechariah. Mark Paustian, "Unleashing Our Calling: Today's Christians Find Fulfillment in Their Vocations," Wisconsin Lutheran Seminary Essay File, http://wlsessays.net/handle/123456789/2027 (accessed July 11, 2020).

[61] Quoted in Paustian, "Unleashing," p. 2.

[62] Paustian, "Unleashing," p. 14.

[63] Herman, *Trauma and Recovery*, p. 266.

[64] Herman, *Trauma and Recovery*, p. 156.

[65] The influential author and counselor Diane Langberg lays out two phases of recovery. Phase one features three things: talking, time, and tears. Phase two begins a reversal of the harm caused by the trauma as the survivor looks for loving relationships, purpose, and reconnection with faith. Despite the differences in terminology and number of phases, Herman's and Langberg's recovery models are basically the same. Both emphasize the importance of grieving loss and reframing the event in the early stages, followed by reconnecting with life and relationships in the later stages. Langberg, *Suffering and the Heart of God*, pp. 146-158.

[66] Herman, *Trauma and Recovery*, p. 161.

[67] Van der Kolk, *The Body Keeps the Score*. This is one of Van der Kolk's main contributions to trauma theory. He includes in recovery not just psychotherapy but also work with the body.

[68] Herman, *Trauma and Recovery*, p. 175.

[69] Herman, *Trauma and Recovery*, p. 178.

[70] Herman, *Trauma and Recovery*, p. 212.

reader's guide

1. In the prologue, the author describes a support team to surround the survivor as God brings healing. Who makes up your support team? Who on your team would be willing to discuss your reflections as you read *Deep as the Sea*?

2. In the first letter, "Deep as the Sea," the author describes his journey from distant observer to compassionate witness. Do you identify more closely with the city-woman who feels unseen or the city-woman who has a compassionate witness? Where might you find a compassionate witness who will speak to you and for you?

3. "Reclaiming Our Refuge" addresses the intrusive power of traumatic memory in your life. Mindfulness techniques can be helpful. What makes Christian mindfulness different from secular mindfulness? Answer in your own words.

4. The author claims in "Prayer-Tears" that the United States' culture has marginalized the lament at great cost to emotional health. Write your own lament, including all five parts: address, complaint, request, promise, and praise. Share your lament with God and, if appropriate, with your compassionate witness.

5. In "Near Death, Near Resurrection," the author listens attentively to Paul's trauma story. Have you ever told someone your trauma story after grounding it in the Scriptures and the gospel?
Consider the following options:
   a. Contact your pastor to share with him.
   b. Have coffee with a trusted Christian friend. Tell him or her just how Jesus rescued you.
   c. Write a narrative on your computer or in your journal.
   d. Create art to help tell your story.

6. "Near Death, Near Resurrection" and "What Can You Know?" form a kind of paradoxical pair. What can you know about what happened to you? What may remain hidden from you in the short term? And why can you be content with this hiddenness?

7. In "The Glory in His Shame," the author speaks to the shame you may feel. In fact, shame may very well be the most intense emotion connected to your trauma. It may be so intense that you have never shared with a living person what happened to you. How does knowing that you are the glory of God set you free from shame?

8. "Survivor's Guilt" touches on survivor's guilt and also survivor's shame. What is the difference between them? How does the Satan vs. Joshua incident minister to any guilty feelings you might be carrying?

9. "One Little Word" and "Overcome Evil With Good" both speak to the anger you may be feeling, but they approach the topic from different directions. Which one speaks more powerfully to you? Why?

10. In "Sheep, Dogs, or More Than Conquerors?" the author states that you are defined by the love of Christ more than by any other life event. Why is it so important for you to really get this truth? What are the potential spiritual consequences if you define yourself instead by your trauma?

11. In "Survivor's Mission," the author brings a word to your need for reconnecting with your mission. One way to think about your mission is to start from the end or to work out from the core. Why is the gospel of Jesus at the heart of everything we do? How does imagining the end bring clarity?

12. In "Inscribed," the author talks about the struggle to move from the extraordinary to the ordinary life again. What part of your life needs to be inscribed with the initials HTTL (Holy to the LORD)?

13. In the epilogue, the author shares the theoretical framework for his series of letters. In what stage of healing do you currently find yourself?